"RE'LIZE WHUT AHM TALKIN' 'BOUT?"

"RE'LIZE WHUT AHM TALKIN' 'BOUT?"

Afro-American tall tales in Black English, capturing the essence of the Black experience
Steve Chennault

Copyright © 1980 by Stephen Dale Chennault

Cover Design from
photographs by Shelby McClendon

Exclusive Distributors
Caroline House Publishers
2 Ellis Place
Ossining, New York, 10562

ISBN 0-912216-24-7

Printed in the U.S.A.

All rights reserved throughout the world. No part of this book may be reproduced in any form by any process whatsoever, graphic or retrieval, without the written permission of the Publisher, except by a reviewer who wishes to quote passages in connection with a newspaper, magazine, radio or TV presentation.

TO:
NELL and CHENNIE

"... it is through the process of making artistic forms—plays, poems, novels—out of one's experience that one becomes a writer, and it is through this process, this struggle, that the writer helps give meaning to the experience of the group."
                                    Ralph Ellison

CONTENTS

FOREWORD by Geneva Smitherman, Ph.D. 11
INTRODUCTION by Stephen Tudor 15
FROM JEROME TO GERONIMO 23
ROOM TO MOVE 29
'ME AN' MY WAYS DURIN' AHMY DAYS' 35
AFTER NINE YO' BEHIND IS MINE 47
BO AN' NEM WUZ BAD! 53
VICTORY OR BUST 59
WHEN DUH HAWK BE TALKIN' 65
DAT FLAMIN' BLACK STAR 73
DUH BADDES' DUDE EVAH
PUT ON TWO GLOVES 81
FLIP-FLOP 89
RE'LIZE WHUT AHM TALKIN' 'BOUT 97
TOO MUCH FUN 101
STREET GAME 107
EATIN' CHEAP AN' LIVIN' LONG 113
MOTHA'S DAY FOR BIG MAE 119
A STICK BETWEEN FRIENDS 127
TOJO'S LAST STAND 137
'LUCKY YOU A BROTHA' 143
THE ROCK OF AGES 155

FOREWORD

On July 12, 1979, Federal Judge Charles W. Joiner ruled on behalf of eleven Black children, attending the Martin Luther King Junior Elementary School, who had charged the Ann Arbor, Michigan School Board with failure to take appropriate action to overcome language barriers impeding their equal participation in instructional programs. The language barrier was not the children's Black speech in and of itself but negative attitudes toward Black Language held by teachers and others throughout the educational system. Judge Joiner's precedent-setting ruling had the effect of mandating that school systems must teach Black children literacy in the language of the marketplace, while simultaneously recognizing the legitimacy of Black English.

I was the consultant for the parents and lawyers in the court case. In the course of our two years of preparation for trial, I often spoke of those Black artists whose works bore witness to the soul and vitality of the Black American Idiom. Steve "Schoolboy" Chennault was among the writers I mentioned. For Chennault, like his predecessors in the Black literary tradition, had acknowledged the legitimacy of Black Dialect long before Judge Joiner's 1979 ruling. Right from the very Jump, in his beginning years as a teacher in the Detroit Public Schools and in his early efforts at chronicling the Black Experience, Chennault demonstrated that he had been baptized in the linguistic fire of our people. He has emerged from it to spin an epic of Black Life in *Re'lize Whut Ahm Talkin' 'Bout?*

Experimenting, revising, changing and listening hard. We can see the hand of Dr. Chennault, the careful scholar, working in concert with Schoolboy Chennault, the flamboyant artist, both of them fiercely and beautifully obsessed with apprehending, reproducing and preserving the pulsating consonants and vibrant vowels of Black America. I mean, like, do we be sayin "wid," "wit," "wif," or just plain ol "wi"? In his rendering of the Black Oral Tradition, Chennault had to make some difficult technical decisions—like how to spell thangs like thing; like how to recreate spoken phrases like "Bo an nem"; like how to capture the pungent sting of Geronimo, Chennault's protagonist who advises that "when duh Hawk be talkin, you betta be movin 'o' have you some draw's on, one!" Chennault, the scholar-artist, will move the novice to conclude what the old folks in the field of linguistics been tellin us all along. Language systems, though deeply imbedded through habit, are, in the final analysis, simply arbitrary. And so too are the written forms that represent language systems.

In addition to the sheer fun of reliving life through Geronimo's eyes, then, the stories are an instructive tool for those who would wish to know Black America's lush creative speech rhythms from a more technical perspective. Under skillful guidance and tutelage, Chennault's fiction might even serve as reading material for students who, like the King School children in Ann Arbor, seek to gain literacy through the reaffirmation of Black Language. Which is not to say, obviously, that Chennault's literary voice has produced a linguistic text or a reading series about life in the Black ghetto. Indeed, there are far more of both of these kinds of usually lifeless educational materials than we ever needed. Rather, the technical mastery evident in stories like "After Nine Yo Behind Is Mine" and "Lucky You a Brotha," speaks to us in bold exhortation: language is more than words and sounds—it is personal identity and world view made manifest. Dr. Stephen Schoolboy Chennault, talkin and testifyin to the max, has captured the life-blood of the Black Experience and momentarily suspended it for us to dissect, analyze, examine and, in the process, learn something about both Language and Life.

Geneva Smitherman, Ph.D.
Author of *Talkin and Testifyin: the Language of Black America*

INTRODUCTION

Steve Chennault is an artist of the spoken language. His stories capture the way people talk on the street, in bars, cooking over a hot stove and sitting on the back porch. His sense of the language is complex. Words convey not only their dictionary denotations and connotations (as our English teachers used to tell us); they also carry the burden of our assumptions about life. Two peoples within a single, large society may use the same words but be at cross-purposes. As Chennault's hero, Geronimo says, "Whut be comin' out duh whitey, duh nigguh take it as it come an' wash it aroun' wit' *his* own shit. And when it come out duh nigguh, it ain't duh same as it wuz when it went in...." It is not only inflections and elided consonants that make the language of Blacks different, but different mind sets, philosophies, attitudes towards politics, sex, police power and religion. And that is what you find in Geronimo. Geronimo is a spokesman, a deliverer of the word, and is, as his interlocutor Schoolboy notes, quite eloquent. There are few things Schoolboy enjoys more than to sit back and listen to Geronimo tell a story.

Steve Chennault, the writer, is Schoolboy, the student of Geronimo's, and it is

Chennault's double role as author/narrator to record Geronimo's discourses, just as if Geronimo were a peripatetic Socrates. The role requires that Chennault/Schoolboy record the linguistic character of Geronimo's speech: the subtleties, syntactical usages, tropes, epithets and ejaculations. For this task Chennault has come well equipped, both by nature and by profession. By profession he has been university-trained in the varied disciplines of linguistics and speech. By nature he has a superb ear. He can *hear* the elided consonant, the lengthened vowel, the subtly inflected syllable, and he can translate that into written language with consummate skill. These gifts, joined with his mastery of the short story, enable him to be the ideal recorder of Geronimo's tales.

Geronimo himself is complex. Although he is not educated, he has quite a range of vocabulary. He can—when he wants—use latinisms, and sometimes sounds a little academic, as in the story, "Re'lize Whut Ahm Talkin' 'Bout." But mostly his wisdom is that of a canny observer of life, a man who can think comprehensively about his years of experience, a transmitter of what he has learned about culture from others, and a hard-nosed realist who himself is appreciative of the good things in life when they do come along—such as the young woman who visits him in a snowstorm in "When duh Hawk Be Talkin'."

The setting of these stories—Geronimo's neighborhood—lies in a particular geographical location in Detroit, Michigan. Chennault records the spoken language of that neighborhood, as distinct from any other neighborhood on the East Side and the West Side of Detroit. In this, Chennault is preserving something of the locale, just as Mark Twain did in recording no less than five dialects in the saga of Huck and Jim traveling down the Mississippi. Who else will do the job of capturing these pronunciations and usages before they are lost? Looking back to the country of my own family origins, I note how the language of Wales was preserved for posterity when the Bible was translated into Welsh in the 18th century. That has become the chief record of Welsh as it was spoken then—a much purer tongue than the adulterated version that obtains in this day and age. To those who say that Black English has no standing as a language, and hence only incidental value, a growing number of scholars and literary artists are showing otherwise. As a dialect, or whatever you name it, Black English has a history and a continuity of meaning and philosophy that goes far back through the centuries.

Where, then, does Geronimo find the *range* of vocabulary that he has made his own? Someone might say that Chennault has put some expressions into Geronimo's mouth that he wouldn't have used. And indeed this is a tricky question. In the 18th and 19th centuries Geronimo certainly wouldn't have been exposed to the "media" and might not have had the ability to read. His main exposure to a wider vocabulary than your ordinary, everyday speech would have been in church, where the preacher might have attained to some rhetorical eloquence. But in the last half of the 20th century, Geronimo has been schooled at least through the fifth or sixth grade. He watches TV and movies, and probably reads the papers avidly. He is actually well-traveled, having been in the service in various places in the United States and in Europe. Ordinarily he uses street speech, but he certainly has a much bigger vocabulary and a more sophisticated community of ideas to draw on. So in this way he's different from, say, a Dunbar character, who might be equally as intelligent, but who would have narrower linguistic horizons.

As a member of the blue-collar Black community in his neighborhood, then, Geronimo could be fairly learned, and stay in character. But what about Schoolboy? Schoolboy moves back and forth between his own professional world and Geronimo's neighborhood. Sometimes he comes on strong in dialect, and elsewhere he spouts Standard English by the paragraph. There is a kind of pathos here—a man caught in two worlds, drawn powerfully into the dominant culture, but attracted equally back to sub-national culture of his people, his roots. At the same time it is important that Schoolboy remain linguistically consistent in his role as interlocutor and frame narrator attesting to the credibility of Geronimo's stories within the story. We ought to feel that we know and can count on Schoolboy. In the later stories he becomes not only reporter, but narrator, and proceeds by the interior monologue. I think particularly of the first half of "The Rock of Ages," where Schoolboy himself is the subject and where he develops the symbolism of the thunderstorm and the church window. In more than one way, the diction of Schoolboy's speeches was as complex a problem as that of Geronimo.

Geronimo's adventures may be divided into two kinds. In the first, Geronimo himself is recounting experiences involving characters he has met and places he has been. In the second, Geronimo and Schoolboy are having *discussions*. The conversation is by turns philosophical, bitterly realistic, wittily humorous. Many of the stories are memorable. I'd pick out especially "After Nine Yo' Behind Is Mine," "Bo an' Nem Wuz Bad!" (interesting in the light of Richard Wright's essay about where Bigger came from), " 'Me an' My Ways Durin' Ahmy Days,' " "When duh Hawk Be Talkin'," "Eatin' Cheap an' Livin' Long" (especially the parts about Geronimo's girlfriend), and of course the story about Joe Louis. How many fighters ever had both that devastating right hand and that swift left jab? Not many. There are memorable characters: Geronimo's father and wife and friends. Through Geronimo, the stories speak to our social realities—they are hardly dispassionate. In "Motha's Day for Big Mae" Chennault dramatizes the sometimes harsh nature of the relationship between the Black male and female. On the other hand, the reader begins to have some sense of "ol' man Berry's" slowly dawning sense of appreciation for Big Mae, and of Big Mae's steadfast love for him. This is a classic bar-room story in which death parts the lovers. The bartender Howard is witness to it all.

It is true that Chennault's fiction in this collection has antecedents in the work of figures like Hughes and Dunbar. Afro-American fiction in particular—and one tradition of American fiction in general—

has a population of characters who become the narrators of their own tall tales, wise saws, dialect stories, and folk superstitions. Well, perhaps we can thank our stars that this tradition is alive and well. You should well argue that the further modern fiction gets from old-fashioned storytelling, the more tenuous its hold upon the general reader. In all the arts—dance, music, painting—the great source of revitalization for sophisticated (and tired) forms is a return to folk culture. In Chennault's fiction we have something genuine that exists in an identifiable time and place. There are local characters dealing with experience which is at once local and universal. There are eloquent speakers of an expressive, regional tongue. This is what Chennault has done for his city in the decade of the seventies. If others have done as much in other times and places, so much the better.

Stephen Tudor
Department of English
Wayne State University
Detroit, Michigan
1979

FROM JEROME TO GERONIMO

"Say, man, how you get the name Geronimo?" I asked my good buddy one evening as we sat on our usual bar stools near the jukebox in Stonestreet's Safari Lounge, sipping on the beers I had just ordered from Mose, the bearded barkeeper.

"In duh pool room," he responded quickly.

"Oh, yeah? Here in Detroit?"

"Hunh, hunh."

"How'd it come about? Tell me about it," I said.

"Uh, one day we wuz ovah dere on Warren Avenue shootin' pool fo' money, you know, an' I wuz kickin' ev'rybody in duh butt. I wuz winnin' *all* duh money. I didn't care what dey bet," said Geronimo. "See, I wuz makin' mo' money'n dey wuz, an' I had a pocket full o' bread *all* duh time, even dough I wuz divorced, see. An', uh ... we wudn't playin' no free games

23

... we wuz playin' fo' *money!* So ev'rybody got down on duh table wit' me dat day. Five, ten ... whatev'r dey wanted t' git down fo'. See, dey thought you'd tremble fo' five, ten dollars a game." He took a swallow of beer. "Shoot, I won me 'bout forty-five o' fi'ty dollars. An' a dude who didn't know my name, he said: *'Dat nigguh takin' scalps jis like Geronimo!'*

"I even beat duh house owner," Geronimo continued. "We wuz playin' Sixty-One, an' I killed 'im ... I killed 'im. I didn't 'low 'im t' win. He didn't win one game. I had 'im diggin' *deep* in his pocket ... an' he had a fam'ly t' take care of, you know, ... off his pool room. But I didn't care 'bout dat. Dat wudn't my problem. I had one, too! I had a fam'ly, too! But anyway, dat's how I got my name. An' I foun' out later dat, uh, my real name an' Geronimo mean duh same."

"Is that right?" I said.

"Hunh, hunh," he said. "Yeah, duh name Geronimo is derived from Spanish."

"Yeah, that's right, it is," I said. "When was that, Geronimo? What year was that?" I went on, anxious to learn more.

"Fi'ty-four," he said. "That wuz right after I got my divorce. You see, dudes thought it wuz easy to rememba my name by dat, see. So from dat day on, dat's duh firs' thang nigguhs would say when dey'd see me. Dey'd say, 'Hey, Geronimo!' An' it jis went on an' on . . . an' ev'rybody could rememba Geronimo easier'n dey could rememba Jerome."

"I understand what you mean, because it was a long time before I found out your name, your *real* name. I had to ask you, remember?" I said.

"Yeah, I rememba. You know," Geronimo went on, pausing to light a cigarette, "a broad come lookin' fo' me one time down on 12th Street when Klein's Show Bar wuz dere, . . . when Yusef Lateef nem wuz playin' dere. An', uh . . . she ax duh bartender, said, 'Do you know Jerome?'

"An' duh dude said, *'Who?'*

"She said, 'Jerome . . . Jerome Clark.' She couldn't make duh dude undastan' my name so she said, 'He a lil' short gray-haired fella wit' a big head . . .'

"When she said dat, duh dude said, *'Oh, you talkin' 'bout Geronimo!'* Said, *'I didn't know his name wuz Jerome Clark!'* Said, 'All I ever knew wuz *Geronimo!' Well, actually, he wuz callin' me by my name. He didn't know dat, dough, an' I didn't know it, either* . . . 'til a few years ago, when I ran across it an' foun' out dat Jerome an' Geronimo wuz duh same name when interp'eted, dat is. When duh broad tol' duh dude she wuz talkin' 'bout duh lil' short fella wit' duh gray hair all ovah 'is head, he told her, said, 'Oh, yeah, dat's Geronimo.' Dat wuz in . . . uh . . . in about fi'ty-eight when duh broad went aroun' dere at Klein's lookin' fo' me. Dat's when dey foun' out my name is Jerome. But ev'rybody would rather use Geronimo ... not 'cause it's been said so long, it's jis easier fo' um t' rememba!"

"Right," I said, "and in addition to that, it's easier for them to identify you with it. Because, you see, Geronimo is really an unusual name, especially for a Black cat," I said. "And you sure don't look like no Indian. I would imagine a lot of people don't know your real name."

"Most people don't!" said Geronimo. "Dere's a whole lot o' folks right now ... been knowin' me fo' years ... dey *still* don't know my name. If dey wuz t' heah dat 'Jerome Clark died,' dey wouldn't know dat it wuz me who had died. But if dey wuz t' read in duh paper dat 'Geronimo died,' ev'rybody who knew Geronimo would know dat must mean *me! Yeeeah!*"

"So that's the story on your name, hunh?" I said.

"Yeah, dat's duh story on it. I firs' got tagged wit' it twen'y years ago, when I scalped dem nigguhs ovah dere on Warren Avenue in dat pool room, an' look like Ahm gon be stuck wit' it 'til Ahm in duh graveyard. An' you know," said Geronimo, a great smile on his round face, "I'd even like t' see duh name Geronimo on my tombstone. Like t' see it read somp'n like

this." He reached into his pocket and got a pencil, then he wrote on the napkin in front of him. It read:
GERONIMO
Born in South Akron, Ohio
Known in Maine, Spain,
Hong Kong and Trinidad,
Died in Everybody's Mind

"Think dat would be a nice lil' 'scription sittin' on my graveyard plot?" he asked me, still smiling.

"Yeah, brother," I said, "to me, that really sounds like a truly immortal soul."

ROOM TO MOVE

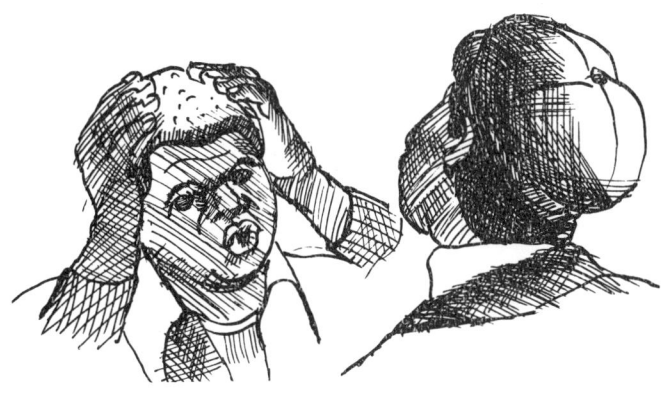

"When some people consider duh brains a person got, dey consider duh masses rather'n duh measure in intelligence dat a head be producin'," said Geronimo with an obvious sense of authority as he arranged his stubby body comfortably on the end of the sofa at my place on that brilliant summer day in August, and sipped gingerly from the tall, too-full glass of gin and tonic I had just fixed him. "You see," he went on in his rather reverent, musical tone like a Black Southern preacher at the start of his text, "dey don't nevah think about the intelligence produced outta duh brain. Dey always look at duh brain an' say, *'Dat nigguh sho got some big-ass brains in dat little-bitty head!'* A-ha-ha-ha-ha-ha-ha-ha-ha-ha-ha-ha..."

He laughed on and on and on. And so did I. Having Geronimo around was like having a steady fire for a sub-zero day in Iceland. He would always light up your soul with laughs. Make tears big as horse turds come to your eyes!

"Yeah, folks always be lookin' at duh size o' duh head rather'n duh intelligence produced out of it," Geronimo repeated. "Like I wuz tellin' ... uh, uh ... ol' Hill ... uh ... Carl ... Carl ... ol' Carl Hill. Now Carl a *crazy* muthafucka! And you know it, and I know it ... and anybody else come in contact wit' 'im know it! Anyway, he come tellin' me, say, *'Man, look at duh shape o' yo' head! You got a greeeat big head!'*

"I told duh dude ... I said: 'Look heah, man, I been blessed wit' enough *room* ... room fo' my brains to function up dere. Dey not all jammed up in no small space ... you can look at my head and see dat!' Den I tol' duh dude, 'I *know* I got enough room wit' dis lil' ov'rlay back heah,' " Geronimo, giggling, went on about his head, his hand patting the three rolls of fat, that "lil' ov'rlay," on the base of his cranium. "Yeah, man, an' I tol' 'im: 'Don't be slappin' me on duh back o' my head, 'cause you messin' wit' my money-maker if you do!' A-ha-ha-ha-ha-ha-ha-ha ... *Dat's my survival kit up dere!*'" he stressed, pointing to his wide moon-shaped forehead. "Ol' Carl, he wuz mo' in'erested in duh shape o' my head dan what be comin' out duh muthafucka... A-ha-ha-ha-ha-ha-ha-ha-ha-ha..."

"That's wha'chu told him, Geronimo?"

"Yeah, Schoolboy, dat's what I tol' dat ol' crazy nigguh! I dug 'im las' Satiddy night, sittin' up dere at duh bar in duh Blue Chip, runnin' his big mouth like he awways do, you know. Outta duh clear blue sky, he went t' talkin' 'bout my head. A jive nigguh. He ain't worth two dead flies wit' dey wings cut off!

"Whenever *anybody* heah me talkin' plen'y shit," Geronimo said, changing the subject a bit, "dat's because my brains got room to move around an' function." He took another sip of gin and tonic. "Dey don't have no pressures on um. Duh only pressures come when I run into dem tough-ass broads out dere... A-ha-ha-ha-ha-ha-ha-ha-ha-ha-ha..."

I poured us both another drink. My stomach, still burning with laughter somewhat, had now begun to knot up with pain. I sat his drink in front of him and continued to listen to his rap. He *really* tickled me with what he had said about the "worth" of Carl.

"Ser'ously," he went on, "it's a damn shame, dough, Schoolboy, 'cause like Jesse Jackson say: 'We have to improve on our lot.' What he mean is dat Black folks done let the fam'ly thang git away from um. Dere's no mo' fam'ly tie ... so *you,* fo' example," said Geronimo, pointing to me, "got to do *all* o' what you got to do, and yet you have to be duh master heah in dis house ... 'cause you duh leader ... an' you have to maintain dat. Y'undastan', 'cause o' duh fact dat yo' wife an' yo' children will lose *all* duh respec' dey have fo' you, if you don't maintain yo' *leadership.* You cain't afford to relinquish yo' leadership as a male, especially as a *Black* male. You have t' hold on to yo' leadership. This is what bring about respec', and also bring about yo' progress. I mean, progress in duh sense where you have nothin' standin' in yo' way, or nothin' workin' against ya. Dis way, you jis keep on movin'. Whatever you concoct in yo' *own* mind to achieve, you don't have much trouble achievin' it, 'cause you got duh equipment to handle it..."

Laughing as I spoke, I said: "You think I got enough room?"

"Evidently, you got enough room," Geronimo said with a giggle in his voice. "You doin' a pretty good job wit' yo' *own* life, an' you takin' care o' yo' family real cool. Don't *mean* dat you gotta have a head look like mine, you know, fo' it to function. When you open yo' mouth and start talkin', I'll know if yo' head got enough room or not. What come out of it let me know if you got enough room . . . or you *ain't* got enough room! A-ha-ha-ha-ha-ha-ha-ha-ha-ha-ha-ha-ha-ha. . ."

'ME AN' MY WAYS DURIN' AHMY DAYS'

"Y'know, duh firs' place I ev'r seen pink sand, natural pink sand," said Geronimo, "wuz in Italy, when I wuz in Reggio Calabria."

"When was that? When you were in the service?" I said.

"Yeah. World War II. We got ovah dere an' had a dumb-ass general takin' us into combat in Italy, an' dat muthafucka couldn't even pass duh combat tes'."

"You kid'n," I said, laughing slightly.

"Dat's duh troof! You see, duh man had money. Dat's why dey made 'im a general ... an' dey put Fort Clark down in Del Rio, Texas ... dey put it on his lan'. Duh government wuz payin' 'im rent fo' dat lan'. General Johnson wuz 'is name. Yeah, man, dat sonabitch went to Washington t' take duh combat tes' an' he failed duh goddamn thang.

"Anyway, we wuz headed t' Italy as a combat outfit, an' befo' we got dere, dey stopped us in Africa an' said, 'Break um up an' make service outfits out of um.' We wuz already infantry, you know, but a horse infantry ... an', uh, dey took duh horses away an' gave us dat dog-face shit. Dem boots an' britches *went!* Yeah, an' duh nex' thang we got wuz some o' dem long pants an' ... an' dem ... wha'chu-call-um ... dey like spats ... uh, leggins! Den we got dem combat boots t' go wit' um. I hated dem muthafuckas, baw, 'cause you had t' lace um up ... an' ev'ry time you went fo' dress parade, you had t' wear um, an' dey had t' be clean. Sheeeeeit," he sighed with disgust, remembering well what he was telling me about his Army days.

"Where were you stationed, Geronimo?" I asked him.

"When?" he responded as he shifted his stubby body more comfortably in the big rocker by the fireplace, and stuck a cigarette in the corner of his mouth.

"Then," I said.

"Oh, I took my basic trainin' in ... uh ... in ACK-ACK ... in Fort Eustis, Virginia," he said, lighting his cigarette at the same time.

"Oh, yeah?"

"Yeah. An' I got a shot at goin' to duh Air Corps. I took a aptitude tes' in Fort Hayes in Columbus ... an', uh ... when dey sent me t' Eustis, dey wuz lettin' dudes out o' Section Eight down in Texas, an' we wudn't hip to it. All dem New York nigguhs wuz gittin' Section Eight like a *muthafucka!* An' when Section Eight needed replacements, dey put *us* in duh muthafucka. Dey said, 'To hell wit' um, long as dey nigguhs! Let duh nigguhs replace duh nigguhs.' An', uh ... dey didn't care 'bout duh fac' dat we'd done had ACK-ACK trainin', you know. Dey jes took us right on out o' ACK-ACK an' put us in duh infantry.

"Anyway, when we went down t' Texas from Virginia, dat wuz somp'n awful, man. I'd nevah been on a horse in my life."

"On a what?" I asked, not hearing him clearly.

"On a horse," he repeated louder this time. "I didn't know how t' ride a horse. I got so' as hell, man, but I learned how t' ride one. I learned how t' post on a horse, an' how t' ride 'im wit'out duh reigns. Dat's how duh Indians ride. Dey don't use no bridle on 'im. Dat's how come a pony so fas' ... h'ain't got no bit to bite on. Ain't nothin' pullin' on 'im t' make 'im have a tender mouth. See, dem bits make a horse mouth tender, 'cause dey keep pullin' at duh corner o' 'is mouth. Dat's how you control 'im. If you want 'im t' stop, jes turn his head from where he cain't see where he goin'. He'll stop

automatic'ly ... thoe yo' ass off, *too,* if you ain't ready. Took me a long time t' learn dat—how t' stop 'im.

"Anyway, when we wuz down in ... uh ... Texas, I got pretty good. I learned how t' ride dem horses 'fo' I left dere. I could post real good. I could ride fi'teen, twen'y miles, posted, you know."

"Is that right?" I said, trying to imagine Geronimo riding a horse.

"Yeah. Y'betta had learned how t' post. If you didn't, you'd have a so' ass when you got back t' camp. I done laid on my belly enough, boy. Shit, I couldn't even sleep on my back. Duh firs' mont' dey had me down dere..." Quickly he seemed to shift his thoughts; he raised his voice as he continued to talk. "Now, I'd done been thu basic trainin', y'undastan'? Now, I had t' go thu *anotha* goddamn basic trainin', *replacin' dem nigguhs gittin' outta dat Section Eight shit!* I had t' go thu duh cavalry basic trainin'."

"What was Section Eight all about?" I said.

"Section Eight? Dem nigguhs wuz *crazy!* You know, undesirables..."

"Ha-ha-ha-ha..."

"You see, if you wuz a Section Eight nigguh, when duh war wuz ovah, you couldn't apply fo' no program dat duh vets got, 'cause you got a *dishonorable* discharge. Dat's what Section Eight wuz—

not honorable! Anythang ain't honorable is *dishonorable!* Regardless o' what terms it wuz gave t' you, unless it wuz medical . . . an' if it wuz medical-connected, it wuz not dishonorable . . . it wuz honorable . . . but it wuz a medical. An' dat wuz duh only one otha'n a honorable dat wuz good. I wudn't 'bout t' come out duh Ahmy wit' none o' dat fake-ass paper shit . . . an' Ahm puttin' my *life* on duh line ovah dere in Italy! Naw-w-w. . .

"Anyway, I wuz slick, man. I wuz like a street nigguh. You know, a street nigguh take chances, baw, an' I took chances. You don't gain nothin' less you take a chance," Geronimo philosophized candidly.

"That's right," I said, realizing the reality of his assertion.

"So duh comp'ny clerk got sick, an' couldn't nobody in duh comp'ny type . . . but me an' him. An', uh, . . . duh First Sergeant tol' me, said, 'You be duh comp'ny clerk 'til duh dude git back from duh hospital.' So, to me, gittin' to be comp'ny *clerk* wuz mellow. All I had t' do, man, wuz sit up dere an' type up all dem reports an' thangs . . . sheeeeit . . . oh, yeah.

"So by time duh dude came out duh hospital, I'd done learned how t' type up dem travelin' orders an' ev'rythang. So I typed me up some travelin' orders t' go an' see a little ol' broad I'd done met up in France when we passed thu dere goin' t' Italy. I wuz in love wit' duh lil' broad, man. She wudn't but seventeen. Her mama had a groc'ry sto' . . . an', uh . . . by her mama havin' a groc'ry sto' . . . uh . . . duh lil' broad wudn't in no poverty . . . an' she didn't have t' deal wit' no soldiers. She had t' 'sociate wit' um, but she didn't have t' *deal* wit' um. Anyway, I got nex' to her, man, an' her mama went t' worryin' 'bout me." He grinned. Then he ran his hand over his round head, and said, "I didn't have all dis gray hair, den, . . . but I wuz *Black!*"

"And her mama went to worrying, hunh?" I said, laughing.

"Yeah, her mama went t' worryin', 'cause duh broad went t' likin' me."

"When was this—in 1940 what?"

"When dis happen, it wuz 'bout time I wuz gittin' ready t' come out . . . 'bout '45 . . . when I wuz gittin' ready t' go back home," said Geronimo. "It wuz duh early part o' '46, 'cause it wuz in duh win'er time. I went up dere t' France an' stayed in duh hotel . . . an' ain't had *nair* money t' pay, but I had cigarettes like a *muthafucka,* baw, an' dem cigarettes wuz jes like money."

"Yeah?"

"Yeeeeah! An' I knew duh ol' broad dat ran duh hotel up dere, see, 'cause she let dem whoes work out duh joint . . . an', uh . . . dey didn't need no pimps, 'cause it wuz a little small city . . . an' she let um turn tricks dere, an' she'd git her percentage out of it, you know. Duh lil' broad I had . . . her name wuz Mickie . . . she duh one introduced me t' duh ol' broad run duh hotel. Duh ol' broad wuz . . . I'd say she wuz 'roun' thirty . . . thirty-two-years-ol'. But, hell, I wuz a young dude, den! *Sheeeeit,* . . . I wuz twen'y-two my *damn* self! *Sheeeeit* . . . I didn't need no ol'-ass bitch, but I come t' find out dat dis ol' broad had some good cock on 'er, boy, an' I said to myself, 'I wanna fuck dis broad.' An' when I did bus' her, I *liked* it! So I *dug* duh broad, man. But I didn't dig 'er tough enough, you know, t' fall in love wit' 'er o' nothin'. I'd jes go on an' buy me some pussy an' git it ovah wit', you know. She said t' me once, said, 'Why you come heah an' you like dat lil' young girl?'

"I said, 'Well, it's like dis heah: Duh young girl ain't nevah been busted out, an' you got some *good* pussy.'

"She said, 'But I don't undastan' why you pay heah, an' you don't fuck ovah dere.'

"I said, 'Well, it's . . . uh . . . a whole lot o' problems dere, if I fuck dere.' She still scratchin' her head t'day . . . if she still livin' . . . an' wond'rin' what duh fuck I wuz tryin' t' say. She thought I wuz tryin' t' confuse her. I wuz jes tellin' 'er like it *wuz!* I said, 'You got a good pussy on you fo' a *ol'* woman,' you know, an' I wuz a young dude, too! An' heah duh otha broad ... duh young girl ... she five years younger'n *me!* Yeah! Sheeeeit! She got a good'n on *her!* Ahm tryin' t' git t' *her* ... 'spite her mama. But duh young girl wo' so many *goddamn* girdles, I nevah could git dem girdles spread enough so I could git my joint hard an' let 'er sit on top of it.

"One day, dough, her mama went to a party, an' I caught duh lil' broad in duh sto' by 'erself ... an' I wish I hadn'ta. Baw, I skint duh *hell* outta my dick! An' dat's when I thought she wuz pregnant. It turned out dat she wudn't, dough, an' I sho wuz glad about dat, 'cause I didn't wanna leave nair drop o' my black blood ovah *dere!* But her mama thought she mighta been pregnant, 'cause duh young girl tol' 'er mama 'bout what happen. So her mama 'fronted me one day. She came down on me ... wanted t' know a lil' bit 'bout my background. Called herself checkin' me. She'd already tol' me she wuz born in duh States. Wuz born in Rhode Islan'. Said she went back ovah dere to France in 1939. Anyway, she said, 'I know you an' Mickie tight. You gon have a job in duh States when you git back home?'

"I said t' myself, 'Oh, shit,' then I tol' 'er, 'Yeah, I had a job befo' I went in duh

Ahmy. I wuz workin' in duh steel mill. I expec' I can git my job back.'

"She said, 'You make much money in duh steel mill?'

"I said, 'Yeah, I make a nice buck. I make enough t' take care a fam'ly. I thank it's a nice buck.'

"She said, 'You know, you duh firs' one dat come thu heah dat's tol' duh troof.' Said, 'All duh res' o' dem nigguhs come thu heah be talkin' 'bout dey daddy got great big farms.' Said, 'But I know dey really talkin' 'bout Mr. Charlie down South.' She said, 'Rememba, I wuz born ovah dere.' Said, 'You know *damn well* I know dem nigguhs ain't got all dem big farms.' "

"That's what she said?" I asked, wondering if Geronimo was really telling the truth.

"Hunh, hunh! So I said, 'I grant you . . . dat's true, but I ain't got nothin' t' lie about. I live in duh Midwes' part o' duh country an' I work in duh steel mill. Dat's whut dey got dere—steel mills—an' I *work* in um!' You see, she wuz lookin' out fo' 'er daughter, 'cause she wuz hip t' duh fac' dat she wuz in love wit' me. I could dance, see, so duh lil' broad *really* fell in love, man. Her name wuz Michele Dhont . . . spelled D-H-O-N-T. I got mail from 'er afta I got home. . ."

"D-H-O-N-T? That's how you spell it?" I said.

"Yeah," said Geronimo. "I got mail from 'er when I got home," he repeated. "I gave her my aunt's address as my mailin' address to make sho I'd git duh mail, 'cause I didn't know whether my mama had moved since duh las' time I got a letter from 'er, see.

"So when I got home ... about a mont' aftawards, a weird thang happen, man. I got a letter from a friend o' Mickie mama ... a lady who lived in a lil' ol' town in Rhode Islan'. Mickie mama had sent her my address. Duh lady said, 'Any time you in Rhode Islan', stop by, 'cause you a friend o' Mrs. Dhont an' Mickie.' Duh letter wudn't wrote like it wuz wrote to a nigguh. Dat's duh reason why she extended duh invitation *straight out* ... like I wuz a whitey, y'undastan'?" He laughed a bit as he kept talking. "I said t' myself, 'If dis black-ass nigguh show up dere, it'll shock duh hell outta dey ass!' She didn't know who she wuz dealin' wit'." Again, he giggled, then he said: "Now whut kinda chance I got goin' thu Rhode Islan', little as it is?

"Yeah, me an' my ways durin' Ahmy days. I rememba Mickie, baw," he said, reminiscing to himself, his eyes off into space. "She wuz a lil' ol' chubby broad ... an' she wudn't real pretty. She wuz jes a nice broad, period! She had a nice personality, an', uh ... she nevah liked fo' you t' force anythang on 'er. An' when she spoke English, she'd try t' speak *perfec'* English ... but she'd speak French befo' she'd speak bad English. An' I tol' 'er, 'Don't worry 'bout it. Make some mistakes!' I said, 'I jes mess-up yo' language an' I don't thank nothin' 'bout it.' " And again, he giggled.

"She'd say," Geronimo went on, " 'Yeah, but you know how t' speak English *well* ... so you should be tryin' t' help me learn it.'

"But she didn't know dat when I wuz wit' 'er I wudn't tryin' t' speak no damn English, I wuz tryin' t' git up unda 'er dress! A-ha-ha-ha-ha-ha . . ."

"Yeah, man," I said, laughing along with him, "I understand wha'chu mean. I guess wars will cause you to be that way!"

AFTER NINE YO' BEHIND IS MINE

One brisk winter evening, when Geronimo stopped by my place after putting in his usual ten hours at the Ford Motor Plant where he worked, I quickly poured him the libations his tastes required: "... a double shot o' Scotch and a short beer." Immediately, he kicked off his shoes, rubbed his hands and wiggled his toes a bit, and got comfortable in the big rocker by the fireplace. He downed the double shot of Scotch and followed it with a long swallow of beer. He cleared his throat with a hard cough, then he said:

"You know, Schoolboy, I don't know why, but for some reason I wuz jis thankin' 'bout how, when I wuz a little boy, my ol' man would act like a *maniac* when he'd be whuppin' me. He'd be beatin' my ass, man! I'd say to myself, 'Dis muthafucka done gone crazy on me ... sheeeeit! Ahma stop dis shit. I ain't gon have duh ol' man beatin' on *me* like dat!' Dat's what I used to say to myself, see. So I decided duh only way to stop dat, man, wuz to stop doin' what he told me to stop doin'. Yeah, . . . *stop dat—whatever it wuz!*"

I could tell from the way he began that the tale he was about to tell was going to be a tickler, so I sat back and tuned in with keen ears. I could feel the humor bubbling up in me.

"I nevah will fo'git it, man. I had a good thang goin' durin' duh Depression," Geronimo began the story of some forty-odd-years-old. "I wuz only about ten, an' I wuz hangin' 'round wit' some *big* dudes. We'd go an' rob dem bakery comp'nies in South Akron. You know, dem bakery comp'nies had dem ol' type doors wit' duh transoms, . . . an' you had to push um open wit' a stick. An' it'd be me an' two o' three dudes six feet tall. Dey'd grab me by the ankles an' shove me up thu duh transom, . . . an' I'd open duh door. Den we'd go in an' clean duh bakery out! We robbed duh bakeries two o' three times, an' dey didn't know *how* dey got robbed. We used t' git all duh cakes an' pies an' put um in some bags. Den we'd go 'round sellin' um fo' ten and fi'teen cent. Some of um would even be broke. We'd have fo', five bags o' pies, cakes, cookies an' shit. We'd done *cleaned out* duh bakery, man. Three times we did dat. So we decided not t' do it no mo', 'cause we felt dey'd be waitin' on our ass if we tried it again. It wuz a chain bakery ... dey had a lot o' stores. An' in all dey stores, dey had transoms."

"You mean like Awrey's Bakery here in Detroit?" I said.

"Yeah. An', uh, ... my ol' man found out I was runnin' duh street wit' five, six dollars in my pocket ... you know?"

"Hunh, hunh."

"My ol' man said to me: 'Where you git all dat money? Shit, I have to work three days ... You doin' somp'n wrong!'

"I said, 'Aw, naw, Daddy, I ain't doin' ...'

" 'Yeah, you doin' somp'n wrong! You got six dollars in yo' pocket, an' you ain't but ten-years-old? Naw, you doin' somp'n wrong!' he said.

"Dat's when he put dat nine o'clock curfew on my ass," Geronimo said.

"Oh, yeah?" I said.

"Yeah, my ol' man told me: 'I don't mean five minutes after nine. I mean nine o'clock!' "

"He did, Geronimo?" I said.

"Sho did, man. An' duh first time, I blowed it, but he let me slide ... I thought I wuz slidin'. He wuz tryin' me to see what I wuz gon do duh next time. So duh next time, I said to myself, 'Well, I got in at nine-thirty the last time.' So I looked at duh clock an' it wuz nine so I started home from where I wuz. I didn't git dere 'til 'bout twen'y after nine. I wuz hustlin' all duh way ... I wuz runnin' like hell! When I got home, my ol' man looked up at duh clock an' said, 'Where you been?' He didn't sound like he wuz mad, an' I wuz *really* happy 'bout dat.

" 'Oh, I wuz up dere playin' on duh playground,' I said.

" 'It's after nine o'clock, ain't it?' my ol' man said.

" 'Yeah. I happen t' look at duh clock an' seen dat I wuz runnin' ov'rtime,' I said.

" 'Well, dat's okay ... you go on an' go t' bed. You got any homework t' do?' he said.

" 'Naw,' I said.

" 'Okay, you go 'head an' go t' bed,' he said.

"I rushed upstairs to go to bed an' my brother told me, said: 'Duh ol' man gon *beat* yo' ass, man!'

" 'How you know he gon whup me?' I said.

" 'You shoulda seen the state he wuz in when it wuz 9:00 an' you wudn't here!' my brother said.

" 'Did he go crazy?' I said.

" 'Boy, he wuz downstairs 'bout to *bust!* He wuz swellin' up! He gon bus' yo' ass wide open!' I wuz hopin' like *hell* my brother wuz jis kid'n me."

By now, of course, my sides were aching with pain from laughing so hard. Geronimo was rolling along at full steam with his boyhood tale.

"At dat time," Geronimo continued, "we didn't have no pajamas t' sleep in ... we'd sleep in our shorts. I said to myself, 'I'll-be-goddamn, if duh ol' man beat my ass, I ain't got *nothin'* to help me.' An' so I didn't have nothin' but duh *bare meat* to give up, y'undastan'?

"Duh ol' man came up dere, boy, an' he turned on duh light in duh room to see if we wuz sleep. He came in dere, man, an' when dat air hit me when he pulled dat cover off o' me, I looked up ... an' dat belt wuz comin' *down!* He said, *'Goddamnit, I don't mean nine-fifteen, nine-twen'y ... I mean nine o'clock! Have yo' ass heah!'*

"Boy, after dat, I didn't care where I'd be! I'd be halfway 'cross duh city an' I'd be watchin' duh *clock* like a hawk! Dudes would be sayin', 'What you keep lookin' at duh clock for, nigguh?'

"I'd say, 'So I can git my ass *home* ... so I won't be gittin' no ass-whuppin'! You ain't gittin' um ... *Ahm* gittin' um.'

" 'Aw, yo' ol' man ain't gon beat ya,' dey'd say.

"I'd say, 'Well, I ain't gon try t' test 'im an' find out. Ahm goin' *home!*

"I stopped dat whuppin' stuff ... an', you know, it made a betta fella out o' me, 'cause after duh War, I went back to Akron, an' some o' duh dudes I'd done went t' school wit'—damn near three-quarters of um done done prison terms by time duh War ended. Ev'ry dude I axed about, he wuz in duh penitentiary, or he'd done did time.

"So gittin' dem whuppins did *me* some good, man. Ahm thankful fo' um! Don'chu thank we betta have a little taste t' dat?"

"Indeed!" I said as I hurried off for the Scotch bottle.

BO AN' NEM WUZ BAD!

"You know, man, when I come along in South Akron, dere wuz some *baaaaaad* nigguhs, boy!" Geronimo said to me as we sat alone at the bar in Stonestreet's Safari Lounge on that Saturday afternoon. As usual, business was slow that day. Only a handful of regulars sat scattered throughout the place. Geronimo downed the double shot of Scotch I had just ordered Mose, the barkeeper, to serve him. Then he went on with what he was saying. "Yeah, duh ones I rememba bes' come outta James Gross' fam'ly ... naw, not Gross ... let me see, what's dey name?" He thought for a few seconds, his head thrown back. "I cain't rememba it, now. Anyway, dey name wuz somp'n like Gross, an' dere wuz a *whole* fam'ly of um ... an' dey wuz all *big* nigguhs, baw, ... an' dem nigguhs wuz *black* an' *meeeeeee-an!* Boy, *dem wuz some mean nigguhs!* Dey'd kick a nigguh's ass in a *minute!* An'

53

dey had a brother name Bo . . . he wuz duh ol'es' one . . . an' dat muthafucka wuz *mean,* boy! An' some dude tol' me, said: 'You betta stop runnin' wit' dem brothers, 'cause you gon wind up in a whole lot o' trouble.'

"I said, 'Well, dey all right wit' *me* . . . dey take care o' *me,* dey don't be lettin' nobody mess ovah *me.*'

"So duh dude said, 'But dey trouble, man. You bet' not let yo' ol' man catch you wit' um!' My ol' man knew 'bout dey fam'ly . . . an' it wuz 'bout seven o' eight of um, you know, an' dey wuz all damn near a year apart . . . an' dem wuz some mean-ass nigguhs, baw, . . . I mean *mean,* Schoolboy. Yeah, I mean, dees nigguhs now'days ain't *nothin'* compared t' dem. . . "

"What would they do, Geronimo?" I said.

"Dey would beat people jis 'cause dey wuz *bad* . . . jis 'cause dey wuz *bad!*" he stressed with an obvious seriousness.

"Just because they could, hunh?" I said.

"*Hunh, hunh!* Dey would run ovah people, man. Ah've seen um . . . seen how dey'd do it . . . how dey'd jis run ovah people, boy, 'cause dey wuz some mean nigguhs, an' nigguhs wuz scared of um. An' dudes would say to me: 'How you run wit' dem little as you is?'

"I'd say, 'Dey don't botha me. Dey cain't git no reputation whuppin' my ass! Dey'd be takin' advantage of a little dude like me, if dey whupped *me!*' An' I tol' Bo an' nem dat, too. So I kept um off o' me when I foun' out I could beat um wit' my brains. Dey stayed off o' me, man. I didn't have no trouble wit' um. I whupped um right quick! I said, 'Y'all cain't gain no reputation kickin' my ass,' an' dey jis laughed an' said, 'Aw, go 'head on, man.'

"But I learned . . . 'cause when I come back from duh War, I said to myself, 'Whew, I'm sho glad my ol' man *did* beat duh shit outta me.' I prob'ly woulda wound up duh same as dem, you know, if he hadn't."

"Just like Bo and them, hunh?" I said.

"Yeah," said Geronimo. "Bo an' nem wuz *bad,* boy. I mean *meeeeeean* nigguhs, boy. Dem nigguhs wouldn't reason wit' *nothin'!* Dey wudn't scared o' duh po-leece o' *nothin'!* Dat's why dey went t' jail, 'cause dey wuz nevah scared o' duh po-leece."

"They were just like that gang here in Detroit a few years ago—'The Black Killers,' hunh?" I said.

"Worse dan 'Duh Black Killers' . . . 'Duh Black Killers' wuz *punks* compared t' *dem!*"

"Really?" I said.

"Yeah, 'Duh Black Killers' ain't nothin' but some jive punks. Bo an' nem nigguhs wuz *bad,* den! Dey couldn't afford t' buy no guns, see. Dey had t' do duh same way dey do now—steal um, an' all *dem* nigguhs had guns."

"Oh, yeah?" I said.

"Yeah! Dat's what made um so mean. Dey had pistols t' back um up, an' dey wudn't scared t' shoot *nobody's* ass. An' dey mammy wuz what made um worse. She condoned ev'rythang dey did."

"Oh, she was one of those kind?" I said.

"Yeah, she wuz one o' dem ol' broads: 'My sons—dey some *bad* nigguhs!' An' folks would say: 'Yeah, dey sho is!'"

"Oh, their mother was like that," I said.

"Yeah, she gloried in duh fac' dat dey wuz some bad nigguhs, you know, an' duh only thang dat made um bad wuz dey wuz carryin' pistols. She wudn't hip to um carryin' pistols, dough. She nevah did see um wit' dey pistols. All she heard about wuz how dey'd be kickin' a nigguh's ass ... an' dey kicked a many nigguh's ass, baw, ... peckawoods, too!"

"Oh, yeah?" I said.

"Aw, man, dey wuz *death* on a peckawood."

"Is that right? What would they do to the peck, Geronimo?"

"Look heah, dey'd gang a peckawood ... an' stomp his ass t' *death,* damn near.

If he crawled outta South Akron . . . alive, dat muthafucka would be lucky, 'specially if he ran 'cross dem brothers."

"Is that right?"

"Oh, yeah. I rememba one dude, he wanted a Black broad. He wuz lookin' fo' a black whoe, you know. So duh dude ax Bo, said: 'Can you tell me where I can find one o' those colored girls?'

"Bo tol' 'im, said: 'Oh, yeah, man, we got some fine bitches down heah, man. I'll gitchu a *fine* bitch. What kinda bitch you want—a light one, a brown one, a black one?'

"So duh white dude said: 'It don't matter, long as she's nice.'

" 'Okay, you wait heah a minute,' Bo tol' 'im.

"So Bo went down duh block an' got his brothers an' tol' um, said: 'Dig, we got one t' go!' Said, 'Now if duh dude got money t' spend fo' a whoe, he got some money on 'im.'

"So Bo came back by hisself an' tol' duh white dude t' come on wit' 'im down dere where his two brothers wuz at. Now, dey had t' go thu a alley t' git t' dis broad's house. An' duh whitey, he so hung up on pussy, he went wit' um—thu duh alley. Dey got 'im back in dat alley, beat duh shit out 'im, took *all* his money . . . an' *left* his ass layin' back dere! Wuz damn near dead! Dey didn't wanna kill 'im. Dem nigguhs beat his ass *good*. Dey nevah did see dat muthafucka in South Akron no mo' ... no, no way! He *sho 'nough* foun' out 'bout Bo an' nem. Got his ass *stomped,* lookin' fo' a colored girl. Yeah, he foun' one..."

VICTORY OR BUST

Geronimo leaned far to his left and slapped hard on the bar two or three times to get the attention of Charlene, the shapely chestnut-colored barmaid standing at the cash register, ringing up a tab. "Gi' us two mo', sweetie!" he yelled.

"Comin' right up, Geronimo," she responded without turning to look up from the money she was counting.

"Charlene sho got a mella turd cuttuh on 'er, don't she, man?" Geronimo, a big smile on his face, whispered to me out of the side of his mouth, his eyes focused on the barmaid's butt as she continued to stand at the cash register. "Yeah, man, she got it all! Got duh three b's—brains, beauty an' booty!" Geronimo emphasized with a laugh.

"Yeah, she got it together, brotha. Ain't no question 'bout it," I assured him.

He giggled a bit, then he said: "Well, ain't no need in me thinkin' 'bout gittin' hol' o' somp'n I *know* I ain't gon wanna cut loose." And, again, he chuckled. Then he said, " 'Cause I know me, man. If I got hol' to 'er, baw, I'd be like a one-eyed cat in a seafood sto', o' a blind dog in a meat shop, one . . . a-ha-ha-ha-ha-ha. . . ' "

"I can understand wha'chu mean. Yeah, she's really a rare breed," I said.

He cleared his throat with a hard cough. "In duh meanwhile, dough," he said, "let me git on back t' duh ranch . . . back t' whutevah dat wuz I wuz talkin' 'bout befo' sweet Charlene dere made my mind run a mo-jo on my ass . . . a-ha-ha-ha. . . " He stopped laughing quickly and paused for several seconds, thinking to himself, it seemed. Then he said, "Dat's right, I wuz talkin' 'bout nigguhs gittin' dey thang togethuh."

"Yeah, you were," I said, recalling the conversation we were having earlier.

"You know, Schoolboy, when I came along in my young days," he went on with what he had been talking about before the sight of Charlene's behind threw him off, "I had it pretty damn good. I didn't have t' fight t' integrate. I didn't have t' fight t' go t' school. An' now Ahm sixty-years-ol'! Y'undastan'? I had it pretty good. But duh white man wuz so far ahead o' duh nigguh den, it didn't mattuh no way," he said.

"Yeah?" I said.

"Yeah, he wuz. See, nigguhs wudn't really no where in sight, 'cause dey had jis come outta slav'ry, y'undastan'? Well, jis figure, at duh turn o' duh cent'ry, nigguhs had jis started t' move. An' from eighteen sixty-five to nineteen hundred, dey wuz wand'rin' jis like duh chil'ren of Israel . . . tryin' t' find um a place t' root! Dey didn't have a pot t' piss in no' a window t' thoe it out of. Y'undastan'? An' dis why so many nigguhs come North, 'cause o' duh Civil War . . . 'cause dey figured dat duh North had mo' freedom.

"But duh North got *less* freedom. Up heah, dey use duh law t' cut down on duh freedom . . . up heah, see. Dey'll take you an' put yo' ass in jail up heah, y'undastan, an' make *money* off you . . . 'cause nigguhs act a fool wit' all dis freedom up heah. Duh white man done jis made a racket out duh thang, dat's all," said Geronimo as Charlene approached us with two frothy mugs of beer. Gingerly, she sat them before us, a cute smile on her pretty face. Then she turned and hurried on away to the opposite end of the bar. Geronimo winked at me in a way that quickly led me to recall what he had whispered about Charlene a few minutes before. I smiled. Then he went on with what he was saying.

"But dem nigguhs fooled dem pecka-woods heah in Detroit in sixty-sev'n.

Messed dey ass up! Sixty-sev'n made hist'ry! Hist'ry, baby! But dat sixty-sev'n thang in Detroit heah wudn't no riot, dough. It wudn't nothin' but a rip-off!"

"Yeah, a Ma'di Gras ... a carnival," I said.

"Dat's all it wuz. Wudn't nothin' sensible 'bout duh sixty-sev'n rip-off. In duh firs' place, dem white cops shoulda nevah took dey ass up dere on 12th Street an' Clairmount an' messed wit' dem twen'y-nine nigguhs in one place, havin' a good time. If twen'y-nine nigguhs is off duh street, an' dey not shootin' an' killin each *othuh,* you s'pose t' leave dem nigguhs alone, no mattuh *whut* dey doin' in dere. If dey tootin' coke an' ev'rythang else ... long as dey ain't shootin' an' killin' each othuh," Geronimo repeated, "let dem nigguhs *alone,* 'cause dey contained in one spot. *It wuz twen'y-nine of um in dere!* Now, dey musta all wanted t' be doin' duh same thang, or dey wouldn'ta been dere," Geronimo figured.

"That's right, they musta been havin' fun," I agreed.

"*Yeah!* Birds of a feathuh flock togethuh!"

"That's right, they do," I said.

"Dat's duh ol' sayin', an' it's true! Birds of a feathuh *do* flock togethuh. An' you know, ev'ry now an' den, a lil' ol' bird'll wanduh away from duh flock an' drif' back, an' duh flock'll say: 'Whu'chu doin' back heah?' An' duh lil' ol' wand'rin' bird'll say: 'Same thang y'all doin' heah—tryin' t' make it. Dat's all. Tryin' t' make it, man,'" said Geronimo in a rather solemn voice. "An' as long as duh flock keep on keepin' on ... keep on keepin' dem *buzzards* off dey ass ... dey'll *make it,* baby. You kin dig where Ahm comin' from, cain'chu, Schoolboy?"

"Yeah."

"Well, let's have a lil' taste t' dat."

"Why not?" I said.

He turned and threw his arm up high, and, with his fist exposing two fingers spread far apart, signaled to Charlene for two more beers.

WHEN DUH HAWK BE TALKIN'

The sudden sound of the whistling wind quickly aroused Geronimo and caused him to focus his attention on the condition of the weather outside. He turned and looked out the window behind him, a frown on his plump face.

"It's gon rain o' snow o' somp'n," he said. "See how it's lookin' out dere. You cain't do nothin' 'bout it, dough," he realized. "All you kin do is sit up heah an' close yo' do's an' do whutevah you can t' keep warm. Dat's *Duh Man* out dere whistlin'. He out dere whistlin' t'day! When He blow *His* whistle, baby, you betta be movin', o' have you some *draw's* on, one! 'Cause it be *col'* heah in Detroit, baw.

"I don't see how dem people live in Montreal. Dey eskimos up dere. Dey *got* t' be. Muthafuckas up dere be talkin' 'bout, 'It's forty-five degrees. It's nice heah.' But dey be talkin' 'bout forty-five below zeero, dough! Forty-five below zeero . . . sheeeeit. If a muthafucka *ax* me t' go anywhere in some weathuh like dat, I'd take me a shotgun an' *shoot duh muthafucka,* an' go t' jail. My boss out dere at duh plant come axin' me once, 'Whu'chu gon do if it git col' enough . . . ?'

"I didn't ev'n let 'im finish whut he wuz 'bout t' say. I said, 'If it *evah* git too muthafuckin' col', I'll be absent from dis job! I'll be *absent!*' Dat's whut I tol' 'im.

"Sheeeeit, don't nothin' but a goddamn fool come out when it be col' enough t' freeze duh air dat you breathe. Ev'ry time you suck in a breath an' it freeze yo' lungs up . . . *dat's a goddamn fool!* Sheeeeit. Any sonabitch oughta have 'nough sense t' undastan' dat! He kin kill hisself! Shoot, man, do you re'lize dat if you go outdo's . . . in forty-five degrees weathuh . . . dat's committin' *suicide!* I ain't talkin' 'bout no forty-five degrees chill factor . . . Ahm talkin' 'bout *forty-five degrees below, period!* Duh chill factor ain't *shit!* When it be dat col', Duh Hawk be *talkin'* t' yo' ass, baw. Dat sonabitch be speakin' real serious t' you. Be sayin', 'Git-duh-hell-off-duh-street-if-you-ain't-got-no-draw's' . . . a-ha-ha-ha-ha . . . 'You-shoulda-saved-yo'-summuh-moneeeey,' " said Geronimo in a high pitch, as if to imitate the voice of the wind. "Dat's whut he be singin' t' yo' ass.

Be sayin', 'Where-is-yo'-summuh-money? You-need-yo'-winter-draw's-on' . . . a-ha-ha-ha. . . ."

"The Hawk be talkin' to you, hunh?" I said.

"*Hawk be talkin', baby!* If you don't b'lieve it, stick yo' lil' narrow ass out dere an' don't have no draw's on . . . a-ha-ha-ha-ha- . . . *you'll gitchu some draw's, den!* A-ha-ha-ha-ha . . . Won't nobody have t' tell you t' go buy none. You'll make it t' duh firs' sto' you kin find, an' you won't be axin' duh man how much dey cos', eithuh. Dey don't cos' too much lessen you ain't got no money. If I got some money, baw, dem draw's gotta be *bought!*

"You know, when I wuz in duh Ahmy, I use t' wear dem ol'-type draw's, wool draw's. Dey go from yo' waist heah," said Geronimo, showing me with his hands on his hips, "all duh way down. An', uh, . . . den dey had a top t' go wit' um . . . you know, two-piece. Wuz all wool! An' dem muthafuckas itch like a sonabitch, baw. Dey got my legs raw, an' dat's why I got sick, from wearin' dem muthafuckas. I said t' myself, 'If I evah git out a uniform, I ain't nevah gon wear no long draw's.'

"When I firs' started workin' out dere at duh plant, afta I got out duh Ahmy," Geronimo continued, "I went t' work one day wit some lil' ol' tight pants on . . . I wuz jis *struttin'* 'cross dat big-ass parkin' lot. Baw, look heah, Duh Hawk come thu dere, Schoolboy, an' hit duh sack o' my nuts, an', baw, I said, *'Aw, my Gawd! Hawk done caught me out heah nappin' an' I ain't ready!'* Man, I wuz *so* damn col'. When dat wind hit my nuts, I turn col' all o-vah! I couldn't ev'n write hardly. I said, 'Let me git duh hell 'way from out heah.' An' soon as I got inside duh plant, in duh back where duh heat at, a dude say, 'Whut duh matta witchu?'

"I said, 'Ahm gon buy me some long draw's *soon as I git off!'*

"I went t' duh sto' an' bought me *three pair o' thermo draw's!'* said Geronimo.

"Did you ask the man how much they cost?" I said, laughing.

"Hunh?" said Geronimo.

"Did you ask the man how much they cost?" I repeated, laughing on and on.

"*Naaaw!* Tol' 'im, *'Jis gi' me three pair! Dat'll hol' me fo' right now!* Ahm gon git some *mo'*, soon as pay day come!' An' afta pay day came, I went back an' got me three mo' pair," said Geronimo.

"Oh, yeah?" I said.

"Yeeeah, sheeeit, an' any time you see me, man, I wear dem draw's 'til I start sweatin' . . . in duh spring. If I take um off any time soonuh, I catch a col', see."

"You still wear um, hunh, Geronimo?" I said.

"Whut, dem long draw's?"

"Yeah."

"Yeah! But you know, when I git off duh job, I come home jis as big an' take um off. Den I put on my pretty clothes an' go on out in duh street wit' my briefs on ... *you know Ahm a damn fool!* A-ha-ha-ha ... Yeah, I take off my long draw's ... done had um on *all* day ... den I put on my briefs, 'cause I be gittin' ready t' go out wit' duh girls! Shit, I ain't gon be caught wit' no long draw's on layin' up in duh bed wit' no bitch! Hell, naw!

"Now, I don't go visitin' in duh winter when it git too col'. Ma Bell work, you know. I kin talk t' dem broads on duh telephone jis like bein' dere. Yeeeeah," Geronimo said in reference to his usual pattern when The Hawk is a little too rough during the winter.

"One day," he went on, "it wuz five below wit' a twen'y-five below zero chill factor outside, an' a broad called me an' said, come talkin' 'bout, 'Don'chu wanna do a lil' business t'night?'

"I said, 'Whut kinda business?'

"Man, I wuz sittin' up in duh mid'le o' my bed an' duh heat wuz jis hittin' me in duh mid'le o' my ass, baw, ... got duh television goin', an' she talkin' 'bout goin' out in five below. I said, 'Girl, you got t' be crazy.' "

"That's what you told her, Geronimo?"

"Yeeeah. I wudn't in'erested in doin' no fuckin' if I had t' go out in all dat shit!

"She come tellin' me, 'Aw, baby, don-'chu want some?'

"I said, 'Yeah, I want some, but I don't want it dat goddamn bad. Dis shit outside gotta git a lil' betta'n dis fo' me t' go out.'

"Nex' thang I knowed, duh damn do' bell wuz ringin'. I said t' myself, 'Now, whut goddamn fool is out heah in dis kinda weathuh?'

"I open duh do' an' dere she stan'. She come sayin', 'Oh, dis my weathuh.' She wuz all bundled up an' ev'rythang. She a heavy ol' broad, too, you know. Dat fat wuz keepin' 'er warm, see.

"So I said, 'Come on in. I cain't heat duh outside.'

"I closed duh do' an' me an' her went on in duh back an' got it on.

"When she got ready t' split, I said, 'It sho is nice . . . nice o' people t' bring pussy t' yo' do' in five below zero weathuh.'

"Now tell me a nigguh as bad as dat—git pussy delivered t' 'is do' in five below!"

"Yeah, that's a bad dude, man," I said, my voice stumbling with laughter.

"Dat's a *meeeeeean* muthafucka!" Geronimo bragged about himself. "Dat's a *bad* dude, man. Any time you kin git a *nigguh!* I can undastan' a white girl goin' out. She lookin' fo' duh beneficials. Ain't too col' fo' her. But fo' one o' dem *Black ones t' come out dere . . . in five below zeero weathuh* . . . sheeeeit. You lucky if you kin talk t' one of um as col' as it is, let 'lone *bring you some!* I said t' myself, 'Oh, Lawd, I must be awfully good,'" he declared, a big grin stretched across his face. "Dat's when I knowed I had somp'n supuh special."

"Yeah, my man, I suppose so, 'cause five below is *cold!*"

DAT FLAMIN' BLACK STAR

"You know somp'n, man, ... *duh Jew git ev'rythang God promised 'im!*" screeched Geronimo, leaning against the parking meter, his eyes fixed on the Star of David chiseled into the dull gray stone facade of the old synagogue—now a Black baptist house of God—across the street from Stonestreet's Safari Bar, the local hangout for the neighborhood drunks and junkies who wander without direction.

"He gets all of what God wants him to have, hunh?" I said, laughing at what Geronimo had just said.

"*Ev'rythang dat God promised him!* Dat's right! All he got t' do is go t' duh Wailin' Wall an' respec' dem holidays ... *respec' dem holidays!* Dem is duh days dat duh Jew give praise t' duh Lawd, y'undastan'? He show respec' ... an' he keep on gittin' money anywhere he go. Ev'rywhere you go an' find a Jew, he got some money. Duh onlyes' way he *ain't* got none, he dead!"

"Ha-ha-ha-ha-ha-ha-ha. . . "

"Dat's right. Dat's duh onlyes' way he ain't got no money. See, he cain't carry it wit' 'im when he dead. Plus, his people ain't gon let 'im take it wit' 'im, anyway. Yeah, he *dead* . . . dat's duh onlyes' way dat he ain't got *no* money. You find a Jew ain't got no money, he a *dead* Jew," Geronimo emphasized.

"See," he continued, "duh reason dat duh Jewish people prosper so well is because o' dey heritage. It's not because o' dey unity so much. If you look back into dey history, you find dat dey wuz jis as disgruntled as we wuz in slav'ry . . . as nigguhs is right now! Y'undastan', all of um don't agree on *nothin'*, . . . but dey foun' out what oppression is when dey went into slav'ry in Egypt. Dey had nevah been oppressed befo' . . . befo' dey wuz *free* people. An' den t' be oppressed . . . an' den t' come outta *dat* . . . an' when dey went out into duh world like duh Lawd tol' um to do, dey prospered. He tol' um: 'Go forth an' multiply anywhere in all parts o' duh world. Multiply an' prosper.' He planted duh seed in *dey* mind . . . to prosper! Dat's why dey awways got somp'n! Dey do what duh Lawd instruct um t' do. Ev'rybody else be sayin', 'Aw, Lawd don't know what He talkin' 'bout . . . ,' "

"How about us, Geronimo? What did the Lord tell *us?*" I asked.

"Look like He ain't tol' us nothin' 'cause we *still* catchin' hell. You see, our problem is dis: We divided . . . an' duh white man know dat. As long as he keep us divided, he can rule us. An' he re'lize dat if we git t' be unified it's gon be hard fo' 'im t' stan' up against us. An' as long as we divided, he kin bounce us aroun' like soldiers . . . put dis one ovah heah . . . put dat one ovah dere, an' so on. You know what I mean.

"See, nigguhs place dey priorities in duh wrong place. Dat's why dey got problems. Duh thangs dat should be done logic'ly, dey don't do it. Dey neglec' t' do dat. An' den dey go an' do somp'n dey ain't had no damn bidness doin', you know. Den duh firs' thang dey holluh is, 'I got a problem!' But dey create duh problem dey damn self! Dey don't face up t' duh fac' dat dey should put dey priorities in duh right place. A lot o' people sacrifice some o' dey principles jis fo' material thangs, an' dat's pitiful . . . dat's pitiful, Schoolboy. It's like cheatin' yo'self. Dat's somp'n Jews don't do.

"Look at it dis way, man: Too many o' our people be tryin' t' keep up wit' dat status quo bullshit dat whitey got. Now, it's true dat we do imitate 'im, but dat don't mean dat we *have* to. It's not

75

compulsory . . . it's only lef' up t' *us*. 'Cause, you know, we got *some* nigguhs who live dey *own* way . . . an' dere's no imitation. Dey live duh way dat *dey* see it wit' what dey *got!* Now, dem people *livin'!* Otha nigguhs, dough, dey jis existin'. All dey doin' is followin' duh whitey, an' duh whitey a damn fool, anyhow, 'cause he got *too damn much!* You see, don't nobody git t' be foolish 'til he git too much. Getty wuz duh onlyes' one I seen who had some sense wit' 'is money, . . . an' dat Howard Hughes wuz a *fool!*

"But, you know, gittin' all dat money ain't what it's all about! It's betta t' be aware o' what limitations dat you have . . . dan t' be fightin' all yo' life an' *not* knowin' dat you got limitations, bein' a po' man . . . 'specially a *Black* one. Dat's hell. A white boy who po' as hell, y'undastan', can lay down an' dream, an' tomorrow dat sonabitch can be a millionaire. He ain't got a damn thang standin' in 'is way.

"But duh judgment day is comin' . . . it is . . . it *really* is. Each time nigguhs achieve a lil' mo' fo' deyself . . . t' dey own satisfaction . . . dey movin' on. 'Cause, you see, what dey friends think about um don't mean shit. What *dey* think ain't *nothin',* 'cause dey opinion don't help yo' household . . . an' it don't tear it down, eitha. But dey *entitled t' dey opinion!* You see, ev'rybody got at leas' two thangs in common—assholes an' opinions, . . . but I don't have t' listen t' dey shit. Yeeeeah, I don't have t' absorb it an' try t' practice it.

"Let me put it dis way: It's like walkin' an' talkin' wit' kings an' queens, an' nevah losin' duh common touch. When you kin do dat, you got a hellava thang goin' fo' yo' ass, 'cause, you see, it's easier t' git along wit' people when you can git along wit' yo'self. I ain't nevah been at war too much wit' myself. I guess 'cause I ain't nevah been a real selfish person. I've awways been outgoin', an' nothin' could harass me, you know, enough t' keep me from thinkin'. I ain't nevah had too many hang-ups about nothin'. I hang loose. I be loose because I be able t' go many places. I can deal. I've dealt wit' educators, doctors, lawyers, realtors, . . . an' I sit down an' hold conversation wit' um. An' when I don't know somp'n, I keep my mouth shut. But what I do know about, I speak on it, y'undastan'? 'Cause soon o' later, it ain't gon all be 'bout real estate . . . we gon have t' move on outside o' dat . . . an' when *we* do, he gon be rappin' 'bout somp'n in my field, den. Yeeeah, I can deal wit' it. It's mellow, man, when you can be accepted on yo' own. You don't have t' preten' t' be *shit!* You can jis go on an' be yo'self, . . . an' if dey don't like it, dat's *dey* problem.

"Like I wuz tellin' you a minute ago . . . 'bout dem people tryin' t' live status quo, like duh whitey. *Dat ain't livin'! Dey ain't ev'n existin'!* Dey jis tryin' t' keep up wit' duh people nex' do'. But you cain't follow duh Joneses," said Geronimo. He quickly stuck a cigarette in the corner of his mouth and lit it.

"I can dig where you comin' from. You're right, it's not hip to be like everybody else," I said.

"Naaaaw!" inserted Geronimo quickly. " 'Cause, you see, if Ahm a individual an' Ahm s'pose t' be dif'ent dan you, Ahm gon *be* dif'ent. If you do somp'n well enough fo' me t' imitate it, den Ahm gon go 'head an' do it an' I ain't gon ax you nothin' 'bout it, 'cause it musta been awful good fo' me t' wanna imitate it."

"That's the truth," I said.

"So," he continued in the same tone of voice, "if I can sit down an' see what it do t' a whitey, see how much his own emotional self destroy hisself, why in duh hell should I follow in his footsteps like a bunch o' cows runnin' ovah a cliff? Why should I try t' imitate 'im? If he wanna go on off duh cliff, let 'im go on off duh damn cliff. But Ahm gon stay back!

"Now, if we wuz like dem Blacks in South Africa, an' didn't have duh education t' cope wit' duh ways o' livin' heah in America, we'd be in trouble . . . jis like dey are. But, uh, dey innocent people an' ain't nevah been brought out duh primitive stage 'til now. You see, man, we got a good three hun'red years start on dem . . . an' as far as Western ways is concerned, we duh baddes' in duh Wes' . . . *we duh baddes' in duh Wes', 'cause we sho 'nough doin' it, baby!* Like dat nigguh I dug duh otha day . . . he rolled up on duh street in a eighty Fleetwood . . . a fo'-do' bro'ham . . . a dark brown one trimmed in gold. Yeah, duh nigguh had 'is order in fo' a *long* time. I said t' myself, 'Dat nigguh doin' it, baw. Dat's a baaad piece he drivin'. He doin' his thang.' I like t' see nigguhs ridin' in dem Cadillacs 'cause it aggrevate dem whiteys . . . let um know dem nigguhs gittin' money. Duh mo' money a nigguh git in 'is hands, duh mo' he can *do*. See, 'cause he been forced t' live cheaper'n any otha sonabitch evah come heah otha'n duh Chinese. Duh minorities awways live cheaper. But, you see, duh whitey be livin' on dat status quo shit. Dey like a junkie. Dey hooked t' it real bad, an' dey cain't cut it loose. Dat's dey jones, . . . an' dey'll have dat jones 'til dey die.

"But t' show we ain't got no hellava jones, we live right up un'neath duh jones, y'undastan', an' we can go eitha way . . . an' it look like we gon beat it, brotha, . . . we gon beat it. We got mo' educated people in duh streets now dan we evah had befo'. Yeah, you cain't quote no time in duh history o' dis country dat dey had mo' educated nigguhs'n dey got right now!"

"You right about that, brotha," I said.

"Yeah, Schoolboy, it's comin' to us, too, jis like duh Jew. We gon git right on top o' duh thang . . . an', baby, when dat flamin' black star fall in our lap, we gon be *leapin'!*"

"Do you think we'll leap high enough?" I said.

"If we don't, grits ain't groc'ry, eggs ain't poultry, an' Mona Lisa wuz a *man* . . . a-ha-ha-ha-ha-ha-ha-ha-ha. . . "

DUH BADDES' DUDE EVAH PUT ON TWO GLOVES

"Joe Louis wuz duh baddes' dude evah put on two *gloves,* baw!" said Geronimo with a stern face as he swayed back and forth in the big oak rocker by the fireplace on that Monday evening at my pad. A cigarette dangling from the corner of his mouth, he ran one hand lightly over his cropped gray hair, then he said, "Yeah, man, any dude dat fought 'im would be half scared befo' he'd git in duh ring wit' 'im, 'cause Joe be knockin' a dude's head *off* . . . be knockin' 'im out in one roun'! Duh dude be sayin', 'Whew! Gawd, I gotta go up agains' dis nigguh!?' He'd be frettin' befo' he go in duh ring wit' Joe, baw! Y'undastan'? An' afta duh firs' jab Joe would thoe, an' *sting* 'im wit' it, duh dude would say, 'Aw, Lawd, let me hurry up an' git dis ovah wit'! Ahm goin' *down* on duh nex' muthafucka he thoe. I ain't gon stan' dis punishment all night.' "

He took a deep draw from the last of his cigarette; then he thumped the butt into the crackling orange flames dancing frantically atop the pile of kindling stuffed in the fireplace. I could sense the design of a master's tale starting to emerge from his lips, so I sat back, crossed my legs and tuned in with keen ears.

"But ev'rybody now'days be talkin' 'bout Muhammad," Geronimo went on, still rocking himself back and forth. "But Muhammad ain't nevah fought nobody, y'undastan'? He fought whut dey had available fo' 'im, see, but as far as matchin' duh calibuh o' dudes dat *Louis fought* . . . ain't no comparison. It took um thirty damn years to admit dat Joe wuz duh baddes' dat evah did it . . . an' dat's not *excludin'* John L. Sullivan . . . an' he wuz fightin' wit' bare knuckles! John L. wuz a bad dude 'til Jim Corbett come along an' beat his ass. Jim Corbett put duh science into boxin' . . . duh dancin' an' duh bobbin' an' duh weavin'. He duh dude dat brought it all in. Diamond Jim. A bad lil' dude. Wuz fightin' heavy weights, an' he wudn't nothin' but a light heavy!" said Geronimo, a glow of excitement scrawled on his round face.

"Yeah?" I questioned.

"Yeah! 'Cause he couldn't git no . . . uh, uh . . . whu'chu-call-um t' stay wit' him!

He wuz too damn good! He wuz kickin' all of ums ass. Wudn't nobody lef' fo' 'im t' fight but Sullivan . . . an' he took duh crown away from *him!* Yeah. Big sonabitch talkin' 'bout, *'Come on! I'm John L. Sullivan! I'll lick any man in duh world!'*

"Jim Corbett said, 'You a lyin' muthafucka. You ain't run up against *me* yet.' Jim Corbett broke dat up! Took dat damn crown away from his ass! An' Diamond Jim would be jis flirtin' wit' duh girls . . . be walkin' 'roun' wit' pretty clothes on an' talkin' plen'y shit."

"Yeah?"

"Yeah! He wuz a flashy dude. He actu'ly wuz duh Muhammad Ali in his time . . . Diamond Jim Corbett.

"But, see, Louis fought muthafuckas dat wuz *fighters!* Max Baer . . . Schmeling . . . muthafuckas dat wuz really down wit' duh science. He wuz taught wit' duh bes'. Duh bes' taught him! Dat's how come he wuz duh champion! Dey talkin' 'bout dey gi' it to 'im. Sheeeit, Joe knocked dem sonabitches *out!* All you have t' do is look at Du greates' fights o' duh cent'ry. *He knocked dem sonabitches clean out!*

"Now, 'Duh Cobra' . . . I knew him person'ly . . . when we wuz in duh Ahmy. I met 'im thu, uh, . . ."

"Who's 'The Cobra'?" I said.

"Ezzard Charles."

"Oh, yeah."

"Ezzard Charles wuz a real nice dude, man. We called 'im 'Champion' in duh Ahmy. Dat wuz his nickname, 'Champion.' Dat wuz duh nickname he had befo' he *really* started fightin'. Afta he started fightin', dough, dey called 'im 'Duh Cobra,' 'cause he'd *sting* yo' ass like Muhammad talked about it. If you don't b'lieve it, ax Joey Maxim what Ezzard Charles do fo' a muthafucka. Yeeeah. He wuz *bad!* Ezzard Charles wuz *bad!*"

"Yeah, he was," I said. "I remember him."

"Yeah, he wuz *bad!* But, see, he wuz followin' duh idol. It's hard t' follow a idol. See, at dat time, Black people's hopes had only moved up t' duh sports field ... an' Joe Louis wuz our champion, only champion we had! Befo' Joe, we didn't have nothin' t' look up to but white champions. Joe Louis wuz duh firs' champion dat come along dat duh race, Black race, united behin', you know. Dey had a champion of dey own! Dey had somp'n dat dey could feel ... all of um wuz a part of it, you know. Dey'd say, 'He a Black man, an' dis somp'n *we* got! Now try t' take dat back, muthafucka!'

"When Joe Louis los' duh title t' Schmeling, mo' bitches cried ... an' nigguhs, too! Yeah! Cried, baw! Wuz like he died! Yeah, it wuz jis like he died, baw, when he los' duh championship. He retired, den he come back. I b'lieve he sol' out, because..."

"Why?" I said.

"Well, see, he wuz knockin' dudes *out*, man, an' dey wanted t' give Lou Nova twen'y-five-thousan' dollars, guaranteed, fo' a fo'-round exhibition wit' Joe. Lou Nova said, 'No, you keep duh money.' Said, 'Ahm too damn ol' fo' a muthafucka like Louis t' knock my brains loose.' Jis thank, duh dude turn down twenty-five-thousan' dollars ... guaranteed fo' fo' rounds! He said, 'Not wit' Joe Louis.' Said, 'Joe Louis killin' people.'"

"Killin' people?" I said, laughing.

"Yeah! He wuz *killin'* muthafuckas, baw. An', you know, dey wuz holluhin' 'bout Joe on duh come-back trail. Lou Nova said, 'Yeah, he on duh come-back trail, all right, an' I ain't gon be one of um!' An' Lou Nova got his brains t'day!"

"Why?" I said with a giggle.

"'Cause he turn dat twen'y-five-thousan' dollars down."

"That's why he got um, Geronimo?" I said, still giggling.

"Dat's why Lou Nova got his brains t'day. An' he tell people dat on television, too! Tell um dat the reason dat his brains ain't rattled t'day is because he didn't fight Louis when Louis wuz on duh come-back trail. Said, 'Why should I fight duh man? I don't need twen'y-five-thousan' dollars *dat* bad.'

"Joe Louis wuz duh baddes' thang dat evah put on two gloves, baw. He'd say, 'Y'all bring um on . . . bring um on.' An' dey did. Dey went an' got ev'ry damn thang dey could *find* . . . ev'n big ol' two-ton Tony, Tony Galento. He didn't ev'n have no bidness in duh ring wit' Joe Louis. He wuz slow an' awkward an' dumb. He knocked Joe Louis down, but he couldn't take advan'age o' dat, 'cause he wuz too damn slow. Joe Louis got off duh flo' an' beat his ass half t' death."

"Yeah?"

"Yeah! He beat Galento up so goddamn bad. Big Tony wuz sittin' up like Humpty Dumpty, wit' blood tricklin' out 'is muthafuckin' nose.

"Den dey went an' got a dude name Unsterdun," said Geronimo, as if he were not sure of the correct pronunciation of the fighter's name. "I don't know how in duh hell he got a championship fight! But he musta been whuppin' dudes, 'cause he wuz a challenger, an' he got a chance t' fight duh champ!"

"Was he German?"

"Naw, he wuz Polish, I think, . . . or Hungar'an o' somp'n.

"Den dey went an' got . . . uh . . . dat big sonabitch from Argentina, an' Joe

Louis killed his ass. Godoy. Arturo Godoy. A big sev'n-foot dude. Joe Louis said, 'Size don't mean shit!' See, he'd done already beat duh shit outta Primo Carnera. Dat wuz duh bigges' sonabitch *evah* wuz champion. Primo Carnera . . . from Italy. He wuz a giant!"

"Well, tell me about Joe Louis and Max Schmeling. Schmeling beat Joe once, right?"

"Yeah, he did. Den Joe turned aroun' an' damn near *killed* dat muthafucka . . . *put 'im in duh hospital!* Beat his ass in less dan two minutes! Sent 'im t' duh hospital wit' broken ribs an' had 'im *sippin' from a quill* fo' one mont'! Yeah!"

"Say what, Geronimo?"

"Yeah, he got his meals from a quill fo' one mont' . . . fo' fo' weeks. He couldn't eat no solid food. Joe Louis put 'im in bad shape. Broke his *ribs!* Joe wudn't gon let dat honkey come ovah heah whuppin' *his* ass. Joe said, 'Ahma show you. Ahma sen' yo' ass back t' Germany!' Hitler wuz talkin' all dat shit, den, you know, 'bout Black people wuz inferior! Joe tol' Schmeling, 'Heah. Now, you take dis back t' yo' *Fuhrer.*' Sent 'im back in a goddamn am'ulance basket! Yeah. Come ovah heah talkin' 'bout he *superior!* Joe tol' 'im, 'I'll show you who *superior!* Dis *ham bone* heah gon show yo' ass who *superior!*' " said Geronimo, shaking his right fist in

87

front of my face. "Yeah, I tell you, Schoolboy, Joe Louis wuz duh baddes' dude evah *put on* two gloves, baw."

"No question 'bout it, hunh, Geronimo?"

"None!"

FLIP-FLOP

"You know, man, my daddy's daddy wuz one o' duh nices' men Ah've ev'r known in my life," said Geronimo softly, reflecting on his grandfather, his feet propped up on the ottoman in front of the fireplace. He went on in the same tone of voice. "Yeah, my daddy's daddy ... dat man wuz so mellow, it's a *shame!* A lot of it's in me ... the niceness, dat is. An' you know, my daddy wuz a good man, so he only passed down from his daddy what his daddy had in him ... an', uh ... I got it from my daddy. Yeah, man, my gran'pa wuz a nice ol' dude. He nevah did say nothin' harsh t' ya, an' all duh time when he'd speak t' ya, he'd awways tell ya somp'n dat make sense ...

"One time I axed 'im, I said: 'Hey, gran'pa, how come we ain't got no money ... an' we poor?'

"He said, 'Well, son, it's like dis: Durin' my time I worked hard an' got a lot o' money, but I los' it all durin' duh Depression. So you jis came along at a bad time . . . dat's all it is to it.'

"Dat's exac'ly what he tol' me. I ain't nevah fo'got dat," Geronimo went on. "You see, my gran'pa had a coal business an' made *lots* o' money, but he los' it all durin' duh Depression when times wuz *hard,* man, . . . an' when it came time t' pay duh government dem damn taxes, he wudn't able t' do it, so his business got wiped out, you know. I use t' sit down an' wond'r 'bout it sometimes. I'd say t' myself, 'How would I be if gran'pa had kept on bein' rich?' I said t' myself, 'You mighta turned out t' be a nasty lil' ol' nigguh.'

"But by me comin' up hard, you know, an' had t' hit duh bottom o' duh barrel an' come back again, I got hip to it, man. I ain't tryin' t' be rich. I got mo' sense'n dat, see. But I'd like t' be rich 'cause it's not somethin' dat would be foreign t' me. You see, I know how t' deal jis like a rich boy do. Only thang is, I know my limitations, as far as finance go. See, dat's duh only thang dat limits me, but I deal jis like a rich boy. My whole life style is jis like a rich boy style. I don't ax nobody fo' shit, I jis go on an' git mine."

"You just go on and cop, hunh?" I said.

"Yeah," said Geronimo, "an' do what Ahma do." He reached for his can of beer on the floor beside his chair. "Dat's what *rich* people do. I know 'bout it.

"A long time ago, my brother ax me a question dat wuz hard fo' me t' answer. He said, 'Man, how do I know all o' dis shit what I be knowin', an' I ain't nevah really been t' school?'

"I said, 'Well, you gotta undastan' dat we come out a rich fam'ly. We wuz jis poor because o' circumstances. But duh quality o' duh fam'ly wudn't broke down.' I tol' 'im, said, 'So if you got people smart enough t' own a big-time coal business an' dey yo' gran'parents, it don't make you no damn dummy when *you* come along.' I tol' 'im, *'I ain't no dummy, am Ah?'*

"He said, 'Naw.'

"Den I said, 'We come off duh same tree, didn't we?'

"An' he said, 'Yeah,' den he paused an' thought fo' a minute an' said, 'Well, I can undastan', now.'

"An' you know, Schoolboy, my brother can *run* some shit t' a nigguh. Yeah, he *strictly* a street nigguh! *Dat's a street nigguh if you ev'r seen one, baw!* An' don't try t' run nothin' ovah 'im, 'cause he know ev'ry game . . . he know duh game dis way," said Geronimo, illustrating a complete circle with his short stocky arms. "He know it *all,* man, . . . duh whole three hun'red an' sixty degrees of it, baw! He know it *all* . . . all o' dat out dere in duh street.

"You see, what happen wuz, me an' my brother did a flip-flop. When I wuz growin' up, I wuz real quiet . . . nevah had nothin' much t' say. I wuz one o' dem . . . wha'chu-call-um . . . uh . . . uh, a introvert, dat's it. I kept ev'rythang inside, see, 'til a speech teacher turn me on. Ev'r since den I been runnin' my mouth. I started flippin' ovah. Soon as I got outta high school an' went on my own, I flipped . . . an' I went t' changin'. I changed my personality altogether . . . flipped. My brother wuz wild when he wuz young, but since he done got t' be a ol' man now, he don't wanna do shit, you know, 'cause he done done it all. He walk aroun' right now wit' three o' fo' thousan' dollars in 'is pocket . . . like it ain't shit, you know."

"He's used to it, hunh?" I said.

"Yeah. Well, he work fo' it, dough, you know," said Geronimo, "but he jis don't spen' 'is money. He keep his business straight. He rely mo' on his physical attributes t' git 'im ovah. Now, he a good strong nigguh, you know, as far as health go . . . an' he ain't been sick in a long time. He had water on duh knee once, but dat's 'bout duh onlyes' thang I know dat he's had. He one o' duh safes' nigguhs you can count on . . . an' he stingy'n a *muthafucka!* Y'undastan', he tighter'n Dick's hat ban'. I awways be tellin' 'im,

'Why you be so goddamn tight? You ain't gon live fo'ev'r, nigguh!' He a lot like me, but I got a lil' mo' polish'n he got, 'cause I got mo' education'n he got ... academic-'ly, dat is. He got mo' street education dan I got, but I got *enough!* 'Cause, you see, I knew how to mellow my education wit' duh street. By bein' in duh street an' comin' out duh street ... an' *gittin'* duh education, I knew how t' mellow it all an' put it t' use ... an' make it work ... an' it *work,* baby. I be way ahead o' most muthafuckas who go t' college. Dey be in school fo' fo' years tryin' t' learn what it took me one year t' learn out heah in duh street. Dey go fo' years t' learn dat, an' when dey git out dey don't ev'n know how t' do what dey went t' school t' learn. Dey gotta have somebody to teach dey ass when dey git out *heah* ... out heah in dis street, dat is. 'Cause, see, a lot of um be runnin' dat academic shit, an' dey don't know, it don't work like dat. 'Cause dig, man, when a muthafucka go t' runnin' it down about his belly growlin' ... dey gon cut off 'is gas ... an' he gittin' laid off duh nex' week, you know damn well he don't wanna heah no academic shit. What he wanna know is how t' git some money! He be tryin' t' git some money t' git duh *gas* back on so he can buy 'im some damn food ... so he can keep on *goin'!* You see, dis kinda thang shock a college student,

'cause o' duh fac' dat he jis come outta duh academic school o' learnin' ... an' he don't really know how to relate t' what he got t' do ... 'cause he ain't had no trainin' in it. So I thank people should be taught in duh street firs' ... an' *den* go into higher learnin', 'cause, you see, den dey'll have a line o' communication wit' duh folks dey got t' deal wit' befo' dey git dey education. In dat way, dey'll know how t' use dey education when dey git outta school. Dis is important fo' nigguhs ... fo' all nigguhs ... fo' dem dat's got, an' fo' dem dat *ain't* got.

"You know, Schoolboy," Geronimo continued quickly, in a way that seemed to suggest that he was convinced about what he was saying, "nigguhs is *slick,* baw. Nigguhs got duh bes' line o' communication of any ethnic group in America. Slav'ry forced um into somp'n dey don't realize dey got ... dat line o' communication. Dat's what Ahm talkin' 'bout! We ain't got no foreign language like duh Europeans who brought dey shit wit' dem. We unique, we ain't got but one language, we like duh Englishmens ... *but we some bad muthafuckas ... ha-ha-ha-ha-ha ... We come from our homeland in chaaaa- ains, man,*" intoned Geronimo reverently, "*in chains ... I mean, chained completely! We done a complete flip-flop,* ... an' now we done mastered duh man's language ... we know how t' deal wit' 'im. You know what Ahm talkin' 'bout 'cause you got a Ph.D. in it..."

"Yeah, that's right," I said.

"An', uh, ain't you jis like me? Ain't you a nigguh jis like me?" Geronimo asked.

"Yeah, man, we the same. You right," I said.

"Same thang ... ha-ha-ha-ha-ha ... so cain't nobody say we ain't doin' it ... ha-ha-ha-ha-ha ... It might not be all thirty million of us, but we sho got some representation," he boasted, his brown face glowing.

"Yeah, you right about that," I said. "Ain't no question 'bout it!"

RE'LIZE WHUT AHM TALKIN' 'BOUT

"You know, Schoolboy, I been thinkin' fo' a long time now 'bout dis Black English thang what ev'rybody be runnin' 'roun' makin' a big fuss ovah dees days," said Geronimo as soon as I slid onto the stool next to him in Stonestreet's Bar that Friday evening, and ordered us a couple of mugs of beer. "Yeah, man," he continued, an unlit cigarette hanging from the corner of his mouth, "I been thinkin' 'bout it fo' a long time, an' I done come t' duh conclusion dat dere ain't no such thang as no Black English . . . dere's only white folks English spoken by Black people usin' duh dialects dat dey lef' Africa wit' befo' dey came heah cent'ries ago as slaves . . . an' dat's why we speak like we do t'day. We take from duh white folks idiom an' change it, an' in turn dey heah it from us an' repeat it deyself. See, when duh nigguh assimilate into dey thang, duh language change. He heah it an' read it as duh lingo be comin' from duh white man," Geronimo declared in his gravelly voice.

"Through his soul . . . ," I began.

"Naw, naw," he cut me off quickly, "not thu his soul. See, whut I'm tryin' t' git ovah t' ya is, when duh whitey speak *his* lingo, whut he be sayin' is duh way his mind be runnin' at duh time, an' it depen' on duh circumstances he be confronted wit'."

Now, what the hell does Geronimo mean by that, I thought quickly.

"He ain't concerned about where duh verb an' shit s'pose t' *go,* y'undastan'? Whut be comin' out duh whitey, duh nigguh take it as it come an' wash it aroun' wit' *his* own shit. An' when it come out duh nigguh, it ain't duh same as it wuz when it went in. 'Cause, you see, when duh nigguh set it out, it come outta dere wit' a dif'ent flavuh an' sound . . . it have to . . . 'cause it be a part o' duh nigguh's dialect, an' dat's somp'n he cain't lose."

"What you mean, then, is that Black folks take the white man's language and put a Black semantic slant on it," I said.

"Right! An' I don't care how proper a nigguh git, he cain't lose his dialect completely. 'Cause, see, long as yo' blood flow in yo' vains, yo' dialect is still dere. You can mastuh anythang, an' assimilate. But somp'n dat's built into yo' genes, it's hard fo' you t' 'liminate it.

"See, basic'ly," Geronimo went on, "dere is no dif'ence between duh nigguh's ideology an' duh whitey's ideology. It's jis a mattuh o' coluh! Dat's duh dif'ence, y'undastan'? Coluh is duh dif'ence between us an' duh whitey, but our ideology in all our idioms is duh same. It's a mattuh o' how duh idioms be presented by duh Black man. Dat's whut make 'im so unique, ev'n dough mos' thangs you see nigguhs do t'day, a white person done already done it. Dat's where nigguhs learned it from in duh firs' place. Where else could dey learn it from? Dey couldn't learn from ovah dere in Africa! Blacks ovah dere got a dif'ent culture dan duh white man in America!"

"So what you're saying is that we have become white Americanized, right?" I said.

"*Yeeeah! You had to become! You wudn't gon leave heah afta duh man gotchu ovah heah!* So you learn duh man's way . . . t' make it easiuh fo' yo'self, see. 'Cause when you know *his* way, you kin deal wit' 'im much mo' betta.

"You see, once a nigguh re'lize whut Ahm talkin' 'bout heah, an' put all dat shit togethuh, den he ain't gon have no problems 'bout whut he wanna do in life. 'Cause, see, den he'll be into his full awareness. Dat's whut it's all about. See, when you become fully *aware* o' whu'chu all about, den nothin' kin stan' in yo' way 'cept yo'self . . . dat's all. Anythang dat you do an' you git a setback on it, it's because you didn't do it right . . . it's *yo'* fault. It's not duh otha person fault. If you try somp'n out an' it fail, dat mean *you* slipped up somewhere on it. So you s'pose t' go back ovah it an' do it again . . . do it *right* duh nex' time. 'Cause, see, persistence bring about achievement," Geronimo rationalized about what he was saying. "Dat's a pretty fancy way t' put it, ain't it? Can you dig it?" He raised his mug and gulped his beer until it was gone.

"Yeah, I re'lize *exactly* wha'chu talkin' 'bout."

TOO MUCH FUN

"*Ge-ron-i-mo!*" shrieked Fuzz as he caught us by surprise when he—in his blue-and-gray postman's uniform, his red beard covering half of his face—stepped onto the back porch at my place on that ninety-degree summer day, and found us sitting there cooling off with one of the two ice-cold six-packs Geronimo had brought with him some ten minutes earlier.

"*How you doin', Fuzzy!? Ha, ha-a-a-a-a...,*" responded Geronimo at the top of his harsh voice.

"Ev'rythang's ev'rythang! What's hap-'nin?" continued Fuzz. He dropped himself into the chair across from us, then he turned to me with: "What's goin' on, Schoolboy?"

"My man, Fuzz!" I returned, glad to see him. "Tell me about it, brother!"

It had been quite some time since Fuzz had been by. His sudden appearance quickly punctuated the scene with a special flavor. With him around now, I knew we would have one of those *mellow* sessions, the kind you really groove on with cats you dig. And the day was perfect for the occasion. It was a lazy day—too hot to do anything but take it slow and cool off. And the soft, warm breeze seeping through the big screen panel seemed to strengthen the mood we all were in. Fuzz's presence, it was suddenly apparent, generated a special charge in Geronimo (not that he really needed it), and got his mouth to running at full speed!

"Fuzzy, . . . hey, Fuzzy," began Geronimo, "you know, I done one o' yo' tricks."

"Hunh?" said Fuzz as he reached and grabbed a beer from the coffee table, and twisted off the cap.

"I done one o' yo' thangs," Geronimo repeated. "You know when . . ."

"You did?" Fuzz interrupted quickly. "Did you have fun?" He laughed. Then he took a swallow of beer.

"Yeah, I *musta* did. I had *too* damn much fun. I tore duh sonabitch up! I carried it too damn far! Ha-ha-ha-ha. . ."

"When you do that?" asked Fuzz.

"Oh, 'bout a week ago," said Geronimo.

"What, your car?"

"Yeah. I got it in duh shop now."

"You didn't hurt yourself, did you?"

Fuzz inquired.

"Bruised my ribs, but I foun' out I wuz in good shape. I went an' got a EKG, a blood test, ... uh, uh, ... a urine test ... ev'rythang."

"Glad you didn't hurt yourself, man," Fuzz said with concern.

"Tell Fuzz how it happened, Geronimo," I said, remembering the details of the accident as he had told them to me just before Fuzz arrived.

"Yeah, okay. Uh, I went to Ellen's birthday party ovah dere ..."

"Who?" asked Fuzz.

"Ellen," said Geronimo.

"At the Blue Chip?"

"Yeah. I went by dere about five o'clock ... five o' five-thirty ... an' I wuz jis sittin' up dere drinkin' ... so I went in duh back an' got me a plate an' stacked up an' greased. Den I went back to burnin' ... an' I burned too much. When I left an' got in duh car, I didn't feel nothin'. I wuz high, but I had it togetha. Anyway, I started drivin', an' I drove all duh way from ... uh ... from, uh ... from Schaefer an' Six Mile to Meyers an' James Couzens, befo' I hit duh damn fire plug. I know I wudn't drunk, dough. If I'da been drunk, I woulda hit somp'n befo' den."

"Ha-ha-ha-ha-ha-ha-ha-ha-ha-ha-ha-ha...," Fuzz and I laughed simultaneously.

"Well, I'm gon tell you, man," said Fuzz as he checked his laughter, "it's that one blink an' yo' eyes don't go back open."

"Dat's what it wuz, Fuzz!" blurted Geronimo, convinced that what Fuzz had said was what caused his accident. "Look heah, I wuz gittin' so sleepy . . . an' I wuz fightin' it so hard. Dat's why I left duh damn party! Anyway, my eyes closed, an' when I opened um back up again, duh car wuz all into duh fire plug . . . had knocked the fire plug ovah, man. Water wuz ev'rywhere! I felt hurt around my ribs, but I didn't know what had done happened, 'cause my eyes went close jis dat quick . . . in jis a second, jis like dat! Good thang I wudn't drivin' fas', you know, 'cause I woulda been sittin' on top o' dat fire plug. . . ."

"Or somp'n worse," inserted Fuzz.

"Right!" Geronimo agreed. "Anyway, I had jis left Six Mile, an' I wudn't drivin' fas', 'cause I'm scared t' drive too fas', anyway, y'undastan'? I wudn't in no hurry. I wuz goin' home, I wuz on vacation, anyway. I wudn't goin' no where but *home*. My prime objective wuz t' git *home!* So I didn't wanna go down on duh expressway, 'cause I didn't wanna run into no damn fool down dere. If I'da done dat, it woulda been two fools down dere—*me* an' *him!*"

"Ha-ha-ha-ha-ha-ha-ha-ha-ha-ha-ha-

ha-ha...," Fuzz and I roared again.

"You see, I'da been a fool fo' bein' down dere!" Geronimo went on, laughing along with us.

"Yeah, it mighta been somebody as big a fool as you down there, in the same shape as you," realized Fuzz, supplying another dimension to Geronimo's story.

"If it'd been datta way, I wouldn't be able t' talk t' y'all today, Fuzz," Geronimo surmised. He giggled and giggled, and we did, too. "Yeah, I'm lucky t' still be wit'chu, fellas." He kept on giggling, then he turned to me and said: "Say, Schoolboy, don'chu thank we oughta have a little taste t' dat? Why don'chu grab a few beers fo' us dere, my boy."

"Coming right up!" I stood up and looked at Geronimo, and said: "A great call, especially for you, 'cause you still here with us, my man, in plain view, same as new. How's that for a little toast to you, brother?"

"Ha-ha-ha-ha ... Yeah, Schoolboy, sound like a *winner!*" Geronimo said, his hand stretched out for me to slap his palm as I dashed off to the kitchen to fetch a few cold ones.

STREET GAME

After putting in many taxing hours at the University one Thursday night, my spirits, somewhat low, were quickly lifted when I drifted into the Blue Bird Lounge for a nightcap, and found my good buddy Geronimo sitting at the bar by himself, nursing a frothy mug of beer, his head bent low, as if to suggest something was troubling his mind. Immediately, I slid onto the bar chair next to him and said: "Hey, dude! What's the deal?"

A bit surprised, he jerked his head quickly and turned and looked at me, a sudden glow surfacing on his round, brown face. Then he said: "Schoolboy! My man! How you doin', brotha?"

"Oh, everything's mellow. How long you been here, man?"

"Only 'bout half a hour." He quickly changed the subject: "You know, man, I jis got thu rappin' wit' a lil' broad . . . she jis left outta heah . . . she wuz troubled, man, an' she a *young* girl. She wanted t' know wuz it necessary fo' me t' have mo'n one woman. I tol' 'er, 'Naw, one woman can do it all. But if one *cain't* do it all, I have t' find it somewhere else ... if it ain't nothin' but a conversation. If she cain't fill up no conversation but she can fill up all duh res', I have t' find me somebody t' talk to.' Dat's what I tol' 'er.

"Den I said, 'I don't mind buyin' a lil' somp'n fo' a woman ev'ry now an' den, eitha. An' if I do *dat,* I do it from out o' my heart ... from feelin'. I don't be buyin' no woman somp'n 'cause she layin' up in duh bed wit' me! I buy her somp'n because o' duh fac' dat Ahm gon enjoy duh damn thang too!' I tol' 'er, 'I don't put nobody ahead o' *me* ... not ev'n my chil'ren! *Ahm number one ... look at me!* I said, 'It's jis like dat record dey got out now about duh man in duh mirror.' I said, 'When you git troubled, go look in duh mirror ... look at yo'self in duh mirror. You cain't cheat on yo'self. Dat's you. When you look at yo'self in duh mirror, you lookin' at yo' true self, *whether you like it o' not!* Dat's all you got. You ain't nothin' but what you lookin' at in duh mirror. You cain't cheat on what you see in duh mirror, 'cause if you do, you cheatin' yo' damn self ... 'cause dat's who in dat mirror, *you.*' Den I tol' 'er, 'So, firs', satisfy thyself an' all otha thangs shall come unto thee . . . an' shall come into place, as dey *should* . . . a-ha-ha-ha-ha-ha. . . ."

" 'Know thyself.' That's what Socrates said, right?" I said.

"Above all otha thangs!" Geronimo screeched in a tonal way. " 'Cause when you know yo'self, you *know* who God is . . . ha-ha-ha-ha-ha . . . *When you know yo'self, you know who God is!"* he repeated more emphatically. He seemed to be winding up like a country preacher. "You see," he went on, "you s'pose t' treat God wit' duh respec' dat you treat yo'self. If you travel thu duh world an' you nevah learn t' 'preciate what God give you, den you'll have a troubled life *all yo' life,* 'cause you ain't doin' a damn thang about tryin' t' overcome *nothin'.* You jis layin' in duh *mud. But you can git up out duh mud! I done proved dat! I got up out duh mud an' washed my ass an' went on steppin'!* Ahm makin' me five hun'red a week. Now, I call dat prolific production. I don't care what you into. It's not so much duh money, but it's nice fo' it t' be convenient t' ya durin' times like what it is now wit' inflation. Yeah, Schoolboy, I be pullin' down five hun'red a week, an' it afford me a *good* livin'. I don't have t' throw it all away, but duh point is dis: Ahm not in no stress an' no strain," said Geronimo.

Then he started counting off with his fingers as he kept talking. "I can pay my bills. I got money in duh bank. If I wanna go any place, I can go any place I wanna go. I got a new car. I can pay fo' it. All I got t' do is keep livin'. Respec' God, an' God will deal *back*. He'll deal it *back! You'll be able t' go out dere an' gitchu somp'n! Dat's what it's all about!* You take care o' what He gi' you, an' it'll take care o' you. You don't need t' worry 'bout nothin' else, lessen somebody off yo' ass out dere in duh street. Y'ain't got no bidness runnin' into dat, dough, 'cause you can keep dat away from you. See, 'cause if you don't 'sociate wit' it too much, it ain't boun' t' happen t' you. I nevah go lookin' fo' trouble, an' I try t' be helpful t' people, y'undastan'. I nevah try to do anythang to regress anybody. If I can help you, cool. If I cain't help you, I'll tell you duh troof . . . I cain't help you. You have t' go an' try t' do somp'n fo' yo'self, see.

"But, uh, . . . you got so many people out dere *lyin'* t' you, you know, an' dey s'pose t' be yo' friend. Dey be lyin' like a sonabitch, man, . . . be lyin' t' yo' face. Dey be tellin' outrageous lies . . . an' duh quickes' way t' git um t' tell a lie is t' ax um fo' some money. If you wanna lose friendship quick . . . wit' anybody, len' um some money . . . len' um some an' you gon lose friendship. I lent a dope dude six dollars a while ago t' git 'im a fix. He needed a fix, but dat's his deal. He a gambler, y'undastan', an' he handle money. Now, I might not see 'im fo' six months, see, but he know he owe me six dollars . . . an' if he don't pay me when I see 'im, Ahma remind his ass, ev'n dough he might not give it to me. But dat ain't gon stop me from gittin' no money. I cain't worry 'bout six dollars when Ahm gittin' five hun'red a week . . . a-ha-ha-ha-ha. . . ."

"Naw, you cain't do that," I said.

"Right. See what I mean? I got t' be worried 'bout goin' t' git dat five hun'red," Geronimo said, giggling. "I might find anotha muthafucka I can buy fo' six dollars . . . ha-ha-ha-ha-ha-ha. . . ."

"Buy him for six dollars, hunh?" I said with a laugh in my voice.

"*Yeah*, 'cause if he don't pay me, dat's exac'ly what I done did, I done bought 'im . . . ha-ha-ha-ha . . . I paid six dollars fo' 'is ass. He cain't ax me fo' anotha dime 'til he gi' me dat six back . . . dat's t' keep 'im off me. But I really don't want duh money back. He kin keep it, but he know he cain't ax me fo' nothin' else 'til he gi' me duh six dollars. Den when he gi' me duh six dollars, he ain't gon git no mo', 'cause he done took too long bringin' duh six back. So I don't have t' len' 'im no mo' money . . . ha-ha-ha-ha-ha . . . See what I mean?"

"Yeah, I see what you mean," I said.

"Yeah. See, Schoolboy," Geronimo went on in a rather slow, deliberate tone, "you learn a whole lot in duh street, man, . . . 'cause dey teach you . . . dey teach you in duh streets, baby. If you ain't equipped when you go out dere an' start dealin' wit' um, you in *trouble!* I tell you, man, dey vultures. Believe me. Dey vultures . . . dey *real* vultures. Dey don't wanna see you do no betta'n dem," he said in a musical way. "Dat's why it's so *hard* in duh street, Schoolboy. It's because o' duh fac' dat each person out dere is doin' dey thang, you know. Yessuh, it's in'erestin' out dere, man. I done been wit' all kinds of people, baw, . . . pimps, dope hustlers, ev'ry damn thang. Yet it don't run me off um, an' dat's how come I know Ahm *strong!*"

"Yeah, Geronimo, you sure seem pretty solid to me," I said.

"Really, man," he responded. Then he threw up his hand quickly and motioned to the barman for "anotha lil' taste heah."

EATIN' CHEAP AN' LIVIN' LONG

Supper was just about to come out the oven on that breezy Saturday afternoon in June when Geronimo dropped by to have a beer with me before dashing off to his job at the Ford Auto Plant where he worked.

"Come on and break a lil' bread with us," I said as I handed him a cold beer. "We gon eat in a few minutes."

"Aw, thanks, Schoolboy, but I jis got up from duh table ovah dere at Mom's Kitchen ... you know, duh joint on Milford. Ahm stuffed, man. Look heah, I had greens, bar-b-qued chicken, 'tato salud, macaroni an' cheese, corn bread, candied yams an' beets ... an' I put a lid on all dat wit' a slice o' peach cobluh an' a big glass o' buttuh milk. So, man, you kin see Ahm tight as a fat'nin hog," said Geronimo, his hands patting his plump stomach. "Yeah, I wuz *greasin'*, baby! Dis beer heah 'bout all I got room fo'."

"What type o' greens you have?" I asked.

"Dey wuz colluds. Had duh fatback swimmin' in um, too! Sho wuz good."

"I've had a taste for some collards for a long time. Think Ahm gon get me some tomorrow," I said, imagining the taste of the greens Geronimo had had.

He took a long swallow of beer, then he said: "Talkin' 'bout greens, let me tell you dis, man. Duh othuh day me an' my ol' lady went t' duh market ovah dere in Highlan' Park. She wanted t' git 'er some turnip greens. When she saw duh price of um, she went t' bitchin'. Come sayin', 'You know, dem greens cos' twen'y-nine cent a *pound!*'

"I tol' 'er, 'It's yo' own damn fault! You an' yo' girlfriends kept on runnin' 'roun' tellin' duh white folks how good duh soul food is, an' now dey done caught on to it. Dat's what run duh price up fo' yuh. Now you cain't eat cheap no mo'. Run yo' *mouf* too damn much!' An' you know, man, dey done gone *clean outta sight* wit' duh price on dem chit'lins. Dem bad boys cos'in' fi'ty cent a ounce, now! It's only 'cause white folks be eatin' um, *too!*

"But still, soul food is duh cheapes' thang in duh market dat we can buy an' git mo' iron an' minerals out of it fo' what duh body need, 'cause duh body is built up o' chemical structure. When you look at all duh stuff you got t' have t' keep you alive, it's all chemistry. Duh meat an' duh bread an' stuff turn into chemistry. It produce duh chemistry inside yo' body. 'Cause if people had t' hol' ev'rythang dat dey ate, dey'd bus' wide open! Dat's why duh chemistry reaction go thu yo' body when yo' food pass thu.

"Now, *we* didn't know fo' cent'ries dat what duh man wuz *forcin'* us t' eat wuz *good* fo' us. All we knowed wuz it kept us alive . . . kept our muscles strong so we could keep on buildin' dis damn country. Y'undastan'? So duh food wudn't doin' us no harm. Musta been doin' us some good, 'cause we still heah . . . an' we *still* strong . . . still strong off dat soul food.

"But *now,* duh honkey done took it *clean outta sight! Yeeeah!* Duh honkey done got duh thang . . . he gon git strong, *now!* 'Cause he done got hip t' dem greens an' corn bread an' pig feets! An' now he know dat's what it take t' slow 'im down from gittin' 'im a early ticket t' duh graveyard! He be sayin' t' hisself, 'How come dees nigguhs live so good an' dey live so long?' Be talkin' 'bout nigguhs don't have duh life span of a white man. Sheeeit, I done seen a whole lot o' nigguhs done out-lived white folks. How 'bout duh dude in duh paper duh othuh day . . . he a hun'red an' somp'n years ol' an' he still votin'. He done had plen'y greens an' ham hocks an' corn bread! He still livin'!"

"Yeah, but he's too old to vote," I said jokingly.

"Must not be. He voted! He made duh newspaper," said Geronimo.

"Still, he too ol' t' vote," I repeated.

"Naw, he ain't! Naw, naw, naw..."

"Well, I'm just sayin' that in the colloquial sense," I said.

"Oh, I see wha'chu mean. You sayin' dat as duh literal colloquial expression," said Geronimo, understanding now what I was driving at.

"Right," I said.

"Yeah, it is a colloquial expression. He is too ol' to vote," Geronimo agreed. "A hun'red years, dat's *too* ol' fo' anythang. Like duh lil' Black girl on TV las' week ... on dat panel show what kids be on. Duh dude wuz tellin' um 'bout science movin' toward duh point where a person can live a span of at leas' a hun'red an' fi'ty years, you know. Dis is duh life time dat dey figure dat duh span can be if dey start preven'ative medicine at a young age, so a person can continue dey life on through ... to a hun'red an' fi'ty.

"Anyway, duh dude axed um, say, 'Would you like to live t' be a hun'red an' fi'ty years ol'?'

"All duh lil' white kids said, 'Aw, naw, I don't wanna live t' be dat ol'. Dat's too ol' t' do anythang.' See, what dey wuz thinkin' 'bout wuz dey pleasures ... figured dey wouldn't be no mo' good by den. Said, 'Naw, dat's too ol'.'

"When duh dude come along to duh lil' colud girl, he say, 'Would you like to live t' be a hun'red an' fi'ty years ol'?'

"She said, 'Yeeeah.' She a lil' young girl, too. Ain't no ol' *woman*. Dis a *younnnng* girl, 'bout ten-years-ol'. Anyway, she said, 'Yeeeah, I'd like t' live t' be a hun'red an' fi'ty.'

"Duh dude say, 'Well, why would you like t' live a hun'red an' fi'ty years?' He acted like he wuz su'prised dat she said dat.

"She looked dead at duh dude, wit' a straight face, man, an' said, 'Because I don't wanna die.' A-ha-ha-ha-ha-ha-ha-ha ... How 'bout dat? Yeah, tol' duh dude, 'I wanna live t' be a hun'red an' fi'ty 'cause I don't wanna die!' Can you dig dat, Schoolboy? 'I don't wanna die.' Out o' duh mouf of a babe came words of wisdom ... duh sho 'nough *troof!*"

MOTHA'S DAY
FOR BIG MAE

"Po' dees nigguhs heah a drank, Howard!" ol' man Berry shouted as expected, his big smile showin' clearly the gold in his top front teeth. He had jes stepped in from the heat outside. "An' when ya git thu, po' um anotha'n!" he added, pointin' to Smitty and Cuz. They had been sittin' at the bar for almos' three hours. Course, wudn't nothin' strange 'bout that fo' them two guys. Sometimes they'd be standin' 'round outside at eight o'clock *sharp*, waitin' on me t' park my ride an' open up the joint. At the same time, both of um said, "Thanks, Berry," without lookin' up from the long list of numbers they were writin' for the first and second races that day. *"Ain't a Jesus, Cuz, if 315 don't fall t'day!"* Smitty yelled out with a laugh. And Cuz laughed, too.

Ol' man Berry limped across the floor to the end of the bar, by the juke box, and grabbed the ripped bar stool, his favorite.

119

He paused and got his balance, then he boosted his little roun' self up onto the stool, quickly crossin' his short, fat legs like he'd always do. I watched him as he wiped away the mucous in the corner of his eye.

"Well, Howard, t'day duh firs' o' duh mont', an' you know, Motha's Day come on duh firs' o' *ev'ry* mont', man!" ol' man Berry giggled under his breath. He hadn't shaved all week long; tiny gray bristles stood out on his jelly cheeks like porcupine quills. Sho did look funny! Course, he always looked funny to me.

"Big Mae still givin' you her money, Berry?" I said with my back turned, as I reached for a bottle of soda to mix Smitty's drink.

"Sho is!" he said like a proud pimp. He cleared his throat with a hard cough.

"She still takin' good care o' ya, hunh?"

"Yeah, Howard, an' she 'bout to come into some *big* dough. Mattah-fac', it s'pose to be comin' any day now." He pulled out a faded twenty dollar bill from his raggedy billfold. "Her sista down dere in Alabama ... I b'lieve dat's where 'tis ... Anyway, she died awhile back an' lef' Big Mae a nice lil' taste o' change ... an' Big Mae say she gon give half of it to me! Dat ol'es' boy o' hers ... June Bug ... You know 'im, don'chu? He duh real quiet one. Ain't nevah got much t' say."

"Yeah, Ahm hip to 'im."

"Well, he duh one s'pose t' come down heah an' tell me right away, if duh money come t'day. Big Mae sho been good to me. Y'know, Howard, life is sweet an' deaf is short! Yeah, Big Mae sho been good to me! Y'know dat, Howard?"

"Yeah, *I* know it, but I wonder if *you* do! I been tellin' you that fo' two o' three years now, but you won't do right. Ain't many women like Big Mae who'd take in a ol' dude like you is, man. Y'ain't got no job. Y'ain't worked since y'all been common-lawin', is ya? How long you been wit' Big Mae now?" I said as I handed Smitty and Cuz they drinks at the same time. I wiped my hands on my apron and reached for the wrinkled bill on the counter, in front of ol' man Berry.

"I ain't gon blow all dat t'day, Howard," Berry said, pointin' to the green bill that I quickly stuck into the cash register.

"Okay, we'll see. That's wha'chu always say." I placed his change in front of him: $17.20. "You been comin' here in the Chit-Chat fo' almos' eight years now, an' y'ain't nevah really lef' out straight yet!"

"I means it dis time dough, Howard, 'cause Big Mae ain't been feelin' too cool heah lately. When I lef' I tol' 'er I weren't gon be gone too long ... Say, whut's dat you wuz axin' me a minute ago?"

"Hunh?"

"Wudn't you axin' me somp'n 'bout me an'..."

"Oh, yeah! I said, 'How long you been wit' Big Mae now?'"

"Uh, ... we been togetha 'bout six years now, I b'lieve..."

"Well, look, how all y'all been able t' git along on that one welfare check ev'ry mont'?" I asked before thinking about what I was really sayin'.

"Shoot, man, dem kids o' hers big enough t' take care o' deyself. Ba' Bruh ... You know Ba' Bruh, too, don'chu? He duh younges'."

"Yeah, I saw him an' Big Mae the other day, pushin' one o' them shoppin' carts down 12th. Look like they was headin' home..."

"Well, anyway, Ba' Bruh got 'im a lil' job shinin' shoes an' sweepin' up ev'ry now an' den at dat bootblack stand nex' to Meatland down duh street dere. Sho is a smart lil' guy fo' 'is age. Ain't but 'bout 'leven o' so!" He handed me a five-dollar bill from the change on the bar. "Gi' us anotha lil' taste, Howard!" said ol' man Berry, again, pointin' over to Smitty an' Cuz.

"Okay, but firs' tell me—how y'all really make it on that welfare check ev'ry mont'?" I asked again. I couldn't see how Big Mae could afford to give Berry money to blow and feed him, too. Plus she had t' take care o' those kids o' hers and pay fo' that small four-room flat all of um lived in 'round there on Pingree. I couldn't undastan' it to save my life!

"Well, I tell ya, Howard, it *do* be hard, *real* hard," said ol' man Berry, shakin' his head from side to side. "But we makes out awright." He looked me right in the eyes, in a way that let me know he *really* knew how hard it was.

"Why don'chu git a job somewhere, Berry? You oughta be 'shame o' yo'self livin' 'round there fo' so long now wit'out workin' *nowhere!* You jes like a parasite!"

"A what?"

"A parasite! You know what a parasite is?"

"Naw-w-w ... don't b'lieve I do." He wondered fo' awhile, then again he shook his head from side to side. "Whut's dat?" he said.

"A bloodsucker! Somebody who live off somebody else! You know what a pimp is, don'chu?"

"Hey, wait a minute now. I ain't pimpin' off Big Mae. She ain't out dere on Twelf Street flaggin' down dem white guys when dey come drivin' thu heah. Dat's duh kinda stuff whut Marcie nem be doin'. I seen her an' anotha lil' chick yestiddy talkin' t' fo' white guys sittin' in one o' dem big white Mercedes, wit' ties

123

on. How 'bout dat, Howard? White on white in white! Nut'n but white! A-ha-ha-ha-ha-ha-ha-ha-ha-ha-ha-ha. . . ." He laughed and laughed and laughed. I did, too, 'cause what he said *was* kinda funny.

"Berry, look, . . . wha'chu doin' is almos' as bad as pimpin'!" I slammed my fist down on the bar. I almos' spilled his drink. I was only tryin' t' make him undastan', 'cause I always did like him. "You *mus'* love Big Mae, don'chu?"

"I s'pose I do. I been livin' wit' her long enough, ain't I!?" he said like he'd given a good enough reason—which, I s'pose, was good enough.

"Well, look, why don'chu try to help that po' woman out, man? You kin git'chu a little work somewhere! I know you can, if you try!"

"You know, Howard, I been thankin' 'bout dat fo' some time now, but ain't nobody got nothin' fo' a ol' man like me to do . . . You know, ev'r since dey cut me loose from dat foundry job I had out dere at Ford's eight years ago, I been jes makin' it duh bes' way I knew I could." He reared back. "Course, duh Lawd know I ain't been quite fair to Big Mae. But I tell ya whut—Ahma go out firs' thang in duh mawnin and find me a lil' work." He smiled. Then he leaned forward and whispered, "I promise ya dis time, Howard. Swear 'fo' God!" He raised his right hand at the same time he spoke. Reminded me of a Boy Scout I once saw on TV salutin' the flag.

"Ah, that's wha'chu said the last time."

"Naw, naw ... I means it dis time, Howard. I really do, 'cause, you know, I wuz jes thankin' 'bout how I owe dat t' Big Mae—an' dem chil'rens, too! She good to me, Howard. She really is, man."

"For some reason I believe you this time, Berry. Don' know why, though."

Smitty and Cuz had split so they could get they numbers in on time. It was almos' one o'clock. The only sound outside was a few cars passin' by ev'ry now an' then. The afternoon bunch—Sam, Marcie, Slim and them—would be comin' in any minute now.

"Thank Ahma head on home, Howard, an' see if Big Mae want me t' do somp'n fo' 'er," said ol' man Berry. He downed the last of his drink and slid off the ripped stool. "I might ev'n take her out fo' a lil' taste later on dis ev'nin', if she start feelin' bettah." He giggled. " 'Cause, you know, Howard, t'day is Motha's Day and I owes dat to Big Mae."

"That's one way to git off to a right start..."

Suddenly a crack of early afternoon sunlight creeped in through the door. Then slowly, real slowly, in walked Big

Mae's boy wit' his head down. I remembered him right away. *He's comin' to tell Berry 'bout that money,* I thought.

"Hi there, June Bug! Wha'chu been up to, Buddy?" I said as he came near the bar. He stopped. He didn't say nothin'. He raised his hand to his eyes. He still had his head down. I wondered, *Is he hurt or somethin'?*

"Say hello, boy! Whut's wrong wit'chu? You know you know Howard!" said ol' man Berry as he reached to pull the boy's hand away from his face. "Whut's wrong? Look heah at me!"

The boy raised his head real slow, but still he said nothin'. His eyes were wet. *Maybe he jes had a fight wit' some o' them little hoodlum-ass nigguhs out there on 12th an' got beat-up.* He jes stood there. Then, like drippin' water from a leaky faucet, a stream of tears trickled down his small, brown face.

"Whut's wrong wit'chu, June Bug? Tell me whut's wrong!" ol' man Berry yelled again. He grabbed the boy real stiff by the collar. *"Why you cryin' datta way, boy? Is ya hurt!?"*

The boy dropped his head again and put his hands over his eyes. Softly, he whimpered as he tried to talk.

"Dey wa-wa-wan'chu t', t' ... come ... ho-ho-ho-home ... Mama dead."

A STICK BETWEEN FRIENDS

Not a light was on in the dingy apartment house on the corner of Pingree and 12th as we neared the walkway to the first step leading to the open door. The fresh rain had just stopped, but the summer heat still hung to the humid darkness. I was afraid. I wanted to turn back but I couldn't; I had promised Willie I would come with him.

As we climbed the broken wooden steps, I slowed my pace and quickly noticed the freshness of the night air. Suddenly, I instinctively imagined the Man was watching us and knew why we were here. I was really scared now and I thought it showed.

I quickly thought of Mama and Daddy. What would they think if they knew I was here and what I was about to do? They would be hurt, very hurt. They had always told me right from wrong, and tampering with narcotics was one of the "wrong" lessons Mama had reminded me of just the week before at the dinner table.

"You stay 'way from those boys who smoke that dope. This neighborhood's become full of that kinda stuff now. Y'hear 'bout it all the time 'round here. I heard that just the other day the police caught some teenage boys up on 12th Street with marijuana. It's a shame. If any of 'em ever approach you, you just walk on away from 'em."

"Ah, Mama, you know I'd never do a thang like that. I got better sense..."

Willie and I had now reached the open doorway.

"I cain't wait to get a stick of gangster, brotha," whispered Willie. "Chappy's stuff is plenty mella!"

I looked at him, not directly, but with a glance. Although a faint smile hung to his dark, pimply face, he too seemed nervous, apprehensive. The sheen in his big Afro gleamed from the bit of light that came from the street lamp in front of the house. He was sixteen, although he looked and acted much older; at least I thought so.

I wondered how long he'd been on the stuff and how it affected him. He never had really told me. I guess I didn't care. I only thought now of how reefer would make me feel. I was curious before, but now I was unsure. Willie had always told me it felt better than our usual high of $.89 wine that we usually drank in the alley with the rest of the cats.

We stepped through the doorway and turned to the first door. Willie said nothing as he quickly knocked. We waited for several moments, then the door opened. A tall fat man about thirty-five stood before us, wearing nothing but underclothing. His undershirt was wrinkled and dirty. His arms and face were wet from the sweat that clung to his body. His huge frame frightened me.

"Hey, what's hap'nin', young blood?" he mumbled to us with a gruff voice as he pulled the door wider so we could come in, and continued to gnaw on the chicken bone clutched tightly in his left hand.

"Ain't nuthin' goin' on. How you feel, Chappy?" said Willie.

"Pretty fair! Been smokin' all day, so you know Ahm in *good* shape! Have a seat, bruh. I'll be back in a minute," said the man as he quickly disappeared into a room at the rear of the hallway.

Not a light was on in the room where we sat. Willie was sitting across from me, but I could hardly see him. The only nearby sound—seemingly from the flat across the hall—was that of Miles, Coltrane, 'Ball and them, penetrating my ears with what I immediately recognized as "All Blues."

Suddenly I felt alone. I was hoping Willie would say something but he didn't. He just patted his foot, keeping a rhythmic beat with Miles' solo. For some reason I was more afraid now than I had ever been.

As I sat there, waiting impatiently, I kept thinking of Mama's brief lecture. Suddenly I felt guilty, real guilty. I knew I had no reason to be there, none at all! It was like waiting for something terrible to happen, but how terrible you really don't know. I became nervous and started biting my lower lip. Then I quickly looked at Willie and stuttered.

"D-D-Dig, man, why don't he hurry up?!"

My voice trembled as I mumbled those words and Willie knew it. I was ashamed, but I didn't care.

"He'll be back in a minute. What's wrong? You scared?"

"Yeah, I guess so. You know, I never did anything like this before, Willie."

"Ah, man, you gon dig it. Jes wait. I remember duh first time I did it. I was a little scared, too. But after you do it once or twice and get good and made, you really go fo' it. Dat's duh troof, brotha!"

"Well dig, man, once you do it, will it make you keep on wantin' it?" I asked like I was convinced now that it would.

"Naw! People don't know what duh hell dey talkin' 'bout when dey say dat."

I wanted to believe him because he was my man. We had been tight since the first day of junior high school when he picked me to be on his side for the three-on-three basketball game that we won. Although we were the same age, he always seemed to know so much more than me. I guess that's why I liked being around him.

Suddenly, a loud, gruff voice echoed down the long hallway.

"Hey, Willie, y'all come on back!"

Willie stood up and gestured, "Come on."

We walked down the dark hall to the last room and turned in. There was Chappy, sitting with one leg propped up on the small kitchen table. A dim lamp hung above.

"Have a seat," said Chappy as he removed his beefy leg and put the sweaty beer can that he held to his thick lips.

A little silver packet with a rubber band stretched around it was on the table among a near-empty wine bottle and a food-stained fork. I stared at it for a moment, then Willie quickly grabbed it.

"Is this for us, Chappy?" he asked.

"Yeah, but y'all gon have to roll it."

"You got some skins, Chap?" Willie asked rather shyly.

"Yeah, right here."

Chappy leaned back in the chair and reached for the small red and white packet of cigarette paper which was on a greasy shelf above his head. He put it on the table, opened it and pulled out several thin sheets.

While Chappy assorted the pieces of paper into two's, Willie removed the rubber band and peeled back the aluminum paper which wrapped the marijuana. I studied both of them very carefully.

"You know how t' twist?" Chappy asked me, as if he knew I didn't.

"No, I don't."

"Well, Willie and me'll do it."

I watched them patiently as I slowly chewed the flavorless gum that had been in my mouth all day. Using their finger tips, they dipped up the green weed-looking tobacco and placed it carefully on the cigarette paper, rolling it tightly and licking the edges. Although they seemed anxious and nervous, they worked skillfully as they hurried to produce the thin white sticks.

"Well, man, dis should do it!" exclaimed Chappy as he twisted the last fibers of marijuana. "I know you gon let me cop one fo' helpin' you roll."

"Sho, Chappy, go fo' yo'self. It's seven here. Dat'll leave three fo' me and three fo' my man," Willie assured him, turning to me for my approval.

"Yeah, Willie, that's right," I replied with a hidden doubtfulness in my voice.

Now was the time and I knew it. Was I or wasn't I going to go through with it?

I thought of Willie again and what this thing meant to him. He seemed to cherish and respect it like some kind of god. I wondered if he was "hooked." I wondered if he wanted me to do it because *he* might be "hooked." I didn't know *what* to think.

Then the thought of Mama and Daddy again! Poor Daddy—he had lost three fingers years ago on the drill press where he worked, but he was still able to hold his job and provide for us in our small five-room house. And Mama—every morning at 5:00 she got up reverently and hurried out to Mrs. Cowan's in Manor Hills where she washed and ironed and house-cleaned for fifty-five dollars a week. She only worked to make sure I'd have enough money to start college after graduating from high school. My finishing college one day was their greatest desire, and they continuously reminded me. It had been very recently that Daddy again had talked about how happy he'd be to see me enter State.

"Well, son, it won't be long now before graduation. If you keep on gettin' the kinda grades you been gettin', you won't have no trouble gettin' in State. Sure would be proud to tell folks 'bout you being there. I'm not worried 'bout you, though. I know you'll turn out all right."

"Sure, Daddy, everything'll work out fine. Don't worry..."

"Here, man," said Willie, pushing three reefers in front of me.

"I think I'll watch you first, Willie," I replied, trying to hide my fear.

Willie looked at me and smiled. He knew I wanted to wait because I was scared.

"Ain't you never smoked gangster, my man?" Chappy asked me.

"No."

"Well, dis some mellow reefa here, brotha. You gon really dig it. Make you feel like you in heaven, walkin' on the sofes' clouds up dere. You gon be high 'n a kite! You'll see!" continued Chappy as he put the slender cigarette to his lips, stood up and left the room.

Willie had already begun. I watched him as he inhaled desperately. I wondered how the reefer was making him feel. He paid me no attention as he continued to smoke. He seemed to crave for every draw.

Suddenly—in almost no time, it seemed—he turned and stared at me. He looked strange. His eyes were glassy and droopy. His hand seemed to tremble as he clutched the burning reefer, putting it to his lips for another draw. A look of pain quickly grabbed his wide face. He placed his hand near the three reefers in front of me and mumbled slowly, "Go ahead, brotha..."

I looked at his face, then at his hand. His hand was still shaking. I put my hand on top of his, relaxing it momentarily. Then I stood up and looked deeply into his glazed, half-closed eyes. He stared back at me with a puzzled expression.

Softly, I spoke: "I cain't cut it, Willie. I'm sorry, man. Ahm gon go 'round on 12th to Big Mama's and get me a hot sausage. I'll wait for you there."

Willie said nothing. He only nodded okay. He looked high, very high.

I turned and walked slowly out of the room, down the long hallway to the front door. I paused for a moment. I guess because I was wondering if Willie was going to be all right. But then I knew he would be.

I opened the door and stepped out, out into the night air. It was moist but fresh.

TOJO'S
LAST STAND

"Goddamn! There go that big black sonofabitch!" I yelled, stretchin' my arm down to the white concrete trash receptacle in front of us. "He in there, I tell you! He in there!" I reached for the bottle of wine on the milk crate behind me.

"I saw 'im, too, Slick! But that ain't Tojo, man! Tojo bigger'n that. Plus Tojo don't be runnin', brotha. He ain't scared o' nobody. You know that, man!" hollered Shaw. "I ain't saw Tojo but two o' three times, but I know that ain't him!"

"I know one thang—if he is Tojo, y'all betta leab 'im 'lone. He might leap out dat thang an' run all y'all nigguhs 'way from dis alley!" shouted ol' man Penn, a grey-headed factory worker who, gigglin', seemed to know for sure that Tojo was vicious enough to kill a rock! "Tojo ain't like duh res' o' dem rats in dis alley. He bigger an' he blacker. Remind you o' one o' dem big ol' over-fed alley cats. But dem

137

cats don't be messin' wit' Tojo, brotha. He don't 'low um 'round heah wit' dat meowin' an' carryin' on."

"Yeah, Mr. Penn, you right! He sho is big—an' he one rat dat's been 'round heah fo' years. I'd spot 'im anywhere, big as he is. Tojo got sen'or'ty 'round dis alley— 'spec'ly in dis area, brotha!" Lil' Willie shouted.

"Well, I tell you what! Ahm gon bus' his brains out his goddamn head when he *do* run out," I said, turnin' quickly to grab a broken house brick near a pile of stankin' garbage stacked up at the rear of the restaurant next door. The smell of the stuff was makin' me sick. "Pull that lid up, Lil' Willie," I went on as I raised my arm and got ready to throw.

"Nigguh, you mus' be crazy! I ain't gon go no where near dat goddamn thang, man," said Willie.

Quickly interruptin', Mr. Penn, rubbin' his wrinkled face, said to me, "Slick, you oughta be 'shame o' yo'self fo' axin' dat boy t' go near dat thang like dat." He laughed a little, then he said, "Ain't no tellin' what might happen."

"Dat's right, Mr. Penn. Tell dat fool!" Lil' Willie grunted quickly as he reached into his dirty blue work shirt pocket and pulled out a crooked Lucky Strike cigaret

"You know, it mus' be hell bein' a rat," slurred ol' man Penn. "Jus' thank—don't *nobody* like yo' triflin' ass."

"Bein' a nigguh's almos' as bad!" Lil' Willie said. "I ain't felt like much mo'n Tojo all my goddamn life!"

"Why you say that, Lil' Willie?" I asked, laughin' at the same time.

"Why? Hell, 'cause I been livin' like a rat evah since I can rememba. Dat's why!"

"Ah, man, thangs ain't been that bad for ya, is they?" I said, still holdin' the raggedy brick as tight as I could.

"I don't know 'bout you, Slick, but fo' me thangs ain't been right in all my thirty-nine years. I been livin' 'round dere on Rochester Street in dat nasty joint fo' ten years now—wit' roaches an' bed bugs an' thangs swarmin' 'round you like you somp'n good to eat."

"You know you lyin', man!"

"Lyin'! Man, I ain't lyin'! Hell, Slick, you oughta know what I mean 'cause where you live ain't no palace, my man. I bet you got dem roaches an' thangs chasin' you 'round, too," Lil' Willie said with a big smile on his face.

"Yeah, I see a roach now an' then, but not the way you talkin' 'bout."

"Hell, sometimes I be scared t' go t' bed, man. Be so many roaches runnin' 'round it make you thank dat if dey *do* 'tack yo' ass you might not wake up duh nex' day."

"Yeah, Lil' Willie, but you ain't nevah saw no rats in yo' joint, though!"

"Saw one once, Slick! Let me tell ya, man. One day my ol' lady fix me a big pot o' black eyes an' a hot pan o' corn bread, you know. An' dig dis heah, man! Jus' as I was gittin' ready t' dip my spoon down in duh bowl, I happen t' look up. Why, I don't know, but I did. Anyway, man, I couldn't b'lieve it. Sittin' up on the kitchen sink wuz a *rat* starin' at my bowl o' peas like he wuz waitin' on me t' offer 'im some. Course, he wudn't near duh size o' Tojo. Ahda died if he'da looked anythang like Tojo!"

"Wha'chu do then, Lil' Willie?"

"Hell, I jumped up like a country rabbit wit' good sense an' got my ass outta dere!"

"Where'd you go?"

"Don't even rememba, man. I do know one thang, dough—I didn't go back t' *dat* joint fo' five days! My ol' lady thought I'd left her ass," giggled Lil' Willie.

"Did she stay there while you was gone?"

"Said she did. I cain't figure out how, dough. You know, man, evah since den I ain't been able t' stan' no rats an' roaches an' thangs."

"How'd y'all ever git rid of 'im?"

"Rid o' who?"

"The rat!"

"Oh, my ol' lady put some o' dat rat-killin' stuff 'round dem cracks an' holes in duh wall while I wuz gone. When I got back on duh scene, his ass had split. Ain't seen 'im since. Hope like hell I don't nevah see his ass no mo'. Course, he mighta packed up an' moved hisself in wit' some o' dem folks down duh hall. Sho hope so!"

I quickly thought about the rat, again. "Tojo still in that garbage can?" I asked Mr. Penn. He'd been starin' at the lid of the receptacle ever since the rat ran in.

"S'pose so, Slick. I been stead'ly watchin' dat lid. Ain't saw 'im run out yet, lessen he got out duh back. Course, he couldn'ta did dat 'cause dat thang's brick, ain't it?"

"Yeah, it sho is," I said. "Say, we oughta burn that muthafucka up! Wha-'chu think, Lil' Willie?"

"Fine wit' me 'cause you know I cain't stan' dem thangs no way! Plus I been diggin' Tojo's ass 'round heah too long now anyway!"

"Well, look, man, you gotta grab the lid so I can throw a match in."

"Okay, Slick, okay..."

Little Willie and I tiptoed up to the big concrete receptacle, makin' sure Tojo wouldn't hear us comin' and try to get his ass out somehow.

"Y'all betta be careful," ol' man Penn warned us, again.

I reached into my pocket and pulled out a book of matches. I turned and whispered to Lil' Willie: "Dig, man, pull the lid up."

Willie put his arm out as far as it would go—till his finger tips grabbed the handle of the lid. Then I lit a match and again whispered to Willie. He yanked the lid, causin' it to flip up and open! I quickly dropped the match down into the paper stuffed to the top. In almost no time fire was jumpin' out all over the place.

"When Tojo come outta there, he gon be a muthafuckin' ghost!" I said, feelin' like I'd set a trap for a wild animal in the jungle.

"Sho will!" said Lil' Willie, puttin' his hand out for me to slap it.

"You nigguhs mus' be crazy if you thank that was Tojo, man," said Shaw who had just got back from the corner drugstore with another bottle of Mad Dog. "If that was Tojo, then that must be his twin brotha over there peepin' at you nigguhs," Shaw went on, laughin' as he pointed to a fat black rat sittin' on the window sill of the restaurant next door, chewin' away on a dried-up orange peel.

My mouth dropped open. I turned and looked at Lil' Willie. All I could find to say was: "Man, ain't that a bitch!?"

'LUCKY YOU A BROTHA'

The blinding rays from the sultry sun, brilliantly yellow in the far-off distance, were emitting ninety-some-odd degrees on that late Saturday morning in July when Boobie and Fathead, in the battered Mustang, turned the corner and pulled up to the burnt-up bar on 12th Street, the car's speakers blasting Wes Montgomery's classic tune, "A Day in the Life." They had just split from Lil' Bit's pad, where they rushed in to drop off and hide the three portable color TV's and two cases of grog they copped earlier from some joints on the East Side.

"Man, duh nigguhs sho did a job t' Twelf Street, didn't dey?" said Boobie, an unusual expression of amazement scrawled on his brown face.

"Yeah, man, sho did!" Fathead responded.

Boobie stretched his big eyes as far as they would go up the long riot-torn street filled with thick smoke and rank odors of burnt rubble. "Look like a black cloud drif'in' in on us," he said as he continued to explore the peculiar details of the grotesque scene.

For some strange reason, though, Wes' tune really seemed hip for the happenings being staged up and down the block. The brothers and sisters—huddled in small, intimate clusters—were laughing hilariously about one thing or another, bragging forcibly to each other over the stuff they had copped the night or day before, and happily sipping wine and grog from clear plastic cups and beer from out the can. The sprightly pageant of Black folks everywhere on the street bore likeness to a band of sea-roving vikings celebrating the brave deeds of unsung heroes just returned from conquest. A few doors away from where Boobie and Fathead were sitting in the red Mustang, near the remains of a beer-and-wine store, a joking voice, rather drunken, could be heard yelling out: *"Inn keeper, inn keeper, mo' wine fo' my mens!"* The only response to the harsh expression was a sudden burst of laughter followed by a woman's voice which laughed: "Aw, nigguh, *please!*"

Just inside the laundromat next to the bar was a tall dark guy with a greasy do-rag tied around his head. He had a young chestnut-colored woman in long, negress braids cornered by a dryer, his right hand massaging her firm, shapely breasts, his left arm wrapped tightly around her tiny waist. She must have really been digging his rap and his game, 'cause *nothing* seemed to be bothering her! Then, too, maybe she was good and high by now and nothing mattered, anyway. Boobie appeared to be mesmerized by her big butt protruding delicately through the tight short skirt she was wearing—and Fathead was captured by it, too!

To the right of the car on the cracked sidewalk—covered with broken glass and trampled shirts and sport coats that some cats probably dropped as they hurried away after looting and burning Esquire Clothiers four doors down—were two little boys tussling over a box of Hershey candy bars which one of them had swiped from Williams' Drugs, the corner drugstore at the opposite end of the block. Yeah, dey copped Doc's joint dis mawnin. Wuz one o' duh firs' ones, too! Jive-ass nigguh! Awways treatin' us like we wuz two dead flies wit' dey wings cut off . . . It seemed the boys were going to fight when the little husky one got his T-shirt ripped—but they didn't. They were quickly calmed down when a fat drunk woman who looked to be about fifty pulled them apart and slurred, "Y'all stop dat foo'ishness! Ain' no need in fightin' ov'r dat candy!

Why don'chu jes split it up!?" The woman snatched the box from the boy's hand and tore it open; then she began counting out the bars: "One fo' you. One fo' you." Finally both boys had their pockets full and looked satisfied. Smiling, they darted away on speedy little feet dodging ugly debris scattered throughout the street, their small fingers stuffing their mouths with broken pieces of sweet chocolate. Quickly, like an unprecedented act of magic, they disappeared into the dense grayish-black curtain of smoke coming from the row of shops two blocks away.

"I got me a taste fo' some o' dat wine back dere," Boobie announced. He quickly cut off the car's motor and threw open his door, hoping that a bit of a breeze would come along and counter some of the devastating humidity now beginning to overwhelm him. He wiped away the many beads of sweat on his forehead, then he reached to the back seat where there were two bottles of red port wine and a quart-sized bottle of scotch.

"It's too muthafuckin' *hot* fo' dat wine, man. Drink it if ya wanna, dough," Fathead said as he, too, reached back and grabbed the green bottle of scotch.

Directly across the street—from the rear of Richstein's Honest Loan Agency, the gutted pawn shop which was still smoldering—a lot of gruff Black voices, only faintly clear, and loud clanking noises could be heard. Gathered there was a small crowd of eight or so young Black men.

"Say, pop, whut's duh deal ov'r dere?" Fathead asked an old whiskered man sitting on a milk crate on the sidewalk a few feet from the car, his thin legs crossed, his back slightly bent.

"Ah, dat's jes a bunch o' triflin' young-ass nigguhs wit' axes an' shit tryin' t' bus' dat man safe op'n." He leaned forward and spit out a stream of licorice tobacco juice at a Budweiser beer can by his foot. His aim was perfect; he hit the tin cylinder dead center!

"Thank dey gon bus' it?" Fathead asked the old man.

"Hell naw!" the old man snapped back quickly. "All dem nigguhs gon wind up in jail o' dead soon as dem polices an' dem Ahmy guys gits heah!" he declared like he knew for *sure* what he was talking about.

Fathead turned to Boobie. "Whu'chu thank, man?"

"I don't know, bruh. Dey might. I know one goddamn thang—we gon sit heah till dey do o' don't," said Boobie, laughing like he always did. He put his sweaty cup to his lips and downed his wine in one quick gulp, a slight frown on his face.

Fathead quickly thought about the young men trying to tear open the thick steel door of the giant safe: Whut would go down if duh Man popped up on duh scene an' saw dees nigguhs 'round dis safe? Would dey shoot dey ass on sight? Would dey herd um up an' take um to duh joint? Whut would dey do?

Suddenly Fathead saw a tall thin brother in a light blue summer suit, standing at the edge of the small crowd of Black men and women assembled near the rear of the red Mustang; he was peeping over his hornrims. He looked out of place. Don't seem like duh type o' dude whut oughta be standin' heah wit' dees brothas and sistas. Look like one o' dem Uncle Toms. Fathead watched him as he reached into his hip pocket and pulled out a folded white hankie to wipe away the sweat on his forehead. When Fathead saw his hands raise a camera to his eye, he *really* thought twice about the young man: He was taking pictures of the burnt buildings and the people mingling freely on the street ... and then he leveled his camera on the band of safecrackers at the rear of the charred shell of Richstein's, the used-to-be pawn shop across the street. Boobie hadn't seen him yet. He was busy watching the big Army tank and fleet of green jeeps cruising down a side street a few blocks away.

"Man, you know," Boobie began, "it couldn't be no worse'n dis in Vietnam.

Dudes wit' machine guns an' thangs, ready t' blow nigguhs away like dey wild game an' target practice an' shit! An' dem tanks an' thangs ...," he continued before Fathead could tell him about the brother with the camera.

"Yeah, man, dat's duh troof!" Fathead returned. "But dig, man, how 'bout dis cat heah from duh press o' somewhere?" Fathead guessed as he pointed gingerly to the young man in the suit so Boobie would know exactly who he was. "He gon take dem flicks o' dem brothas coppin' dat safe right back t' duh white folks an' git *all* dem cats busted. So he a Tom, ain't he?"

"Yeah, you right," Boobie agreed. "He black—but den he ain't black. You know, man, dere's a lots o' Black cats dat way, too! It's a damn shame! Jes thank—some o' yo' own brothas is yo' enemy. Can you dig where Ahm comin' from?"

"Yeah, bruh," Fathead said, feeling he really *did* know what Boobie meant.

Quickly shouting, Boobie said: *"Man, dis dude crazy!* Dat's duh same as havin' a gun on dem nigguhs, man! I could dig it if he wuz a honkey, but he a *brotha—an' duh nigguh blacker'n me!* Sheeeit...," Boobie went on with disgust.

The young man in the blue suit, unknowing of his conspicuousness, loosened his tie; then he shifted his position a bit so he could get better focus on the many sights he was witnessing. Now, in the very hot sun still beaming profusely, he was standing near the front of the small, drunken crowd who had started taunting the exhausted safecrackers—but the safecrackers ignored the drunk voices completely.

"Boobie, look at dat fool-ass idiot!" Fathead declared of the young man in the blue suit. "He got mo' nerve'n duh law allow!"

Suddenly a deep, forceful voice screamed out from the small band of men inside the still-smoldering pawn show: *"Hey, y'all, dig dat dude! Him dere in duh suit! He takin' pictures!"*

"Ah, man, dey done saw 'im!" Boobie shouted, sounding as excited as the voice from inside the pawn shop across the street.

Startled by Boobie's voice, Fathead, his eyes bucked, jerked his head away from watching the frail little girl coming along on the deformed sidewalk, her small hands struggling to lug home the half-gallon of milk she had taken from Fairway Market, the Syrian-run grocery store near the end of the block . . . next to Williams' Drugs, Doc's place. He almost spilled his cup of warm, strong scotch that, along with the unbearable heat of the day, was now beginning to make him sick on the stomach. He belched—and as he did, thoughts of what was about to happen to the young man with the camera raced through his mind.

From the pawn shop the Black safecrackers came running and screaming and cussing like a pack of Indian warriors sieging a fort of Confederate soldiers in a western movie. The young man in the blue suit didn't move! He was scared! The stark horror etched in his chocolate face was plainly clear. Quickly a wet spot appeared all over the inside of his pant legs; he was peeing on himself.

"I tol' you, man! I tol' you!" Boobie asserted sharply, reminding Fathead of what was going to happen when and if the young man in the suit was seen by the safecrackers. Fathead said nothing; he just looked on, amazed.

"Y'all leab dat guy 'lone!" yelled the old man on the milk crate. He was still chewing the tobacco that had probably been in his mouth all day. He reminded Fathead of one o' dem ol' slav'ry-time brothas I rememba learnin' 'bout in dat Black hist'ry class in high school. Nobody seemed to hear the old man, though he hollered at the top of his feeble voice.

"Whu'chu gon do wit' dem pictures in dat cam'ra, muthafucka!?" roared a short, stocky man, his gruff voice, Black with rage, lashing severely the young man in

the light blue suit. Beastly, the stocky man lunged forward, like a panther in disguise, the stiff fingers of one hand sinking dirty nails into the young man's lower neck, the palm of the other slapping sharply the blank face paralyzed with fear.

Then another safecracker filled with fury reached and yanked the camera, ripping it from the strap around the young man's neck. *"Where you from, nigguh—one o' dem newspapers!? You wanna git us busted, don'chu?"*

Still, the young man didn't move. In a soft voice struggling to emerge, he managed to stutter, "Na-w-w-w . . . , I-I-I was jus' takin' pictures for myself."

In the red Mustang, Boobie, almost whispering, asked Fathead nervously, "You don't thank dey gon off duh dude, do you?"

"I don't know. Hope not. He wuz only takin' dey flick," Fathead said, hoping the way he was feeling would help save the young man in the suit.

Suddenly a huge, rough-looking man in a dirty T-shirt, wet with sweat that made the thin fabric stick to his skin, rushed through the circle of safecrackers, shoving two of them aside with his giant arms, and yelled: *"Don't botha 'im! Leave 'im 'lone! He a brotha!"*

"A brotha!? Sheeeit," returned another

one of the safecrackers, a short piece of steel pipe raised firmly in his hand.

"*Wait one goddamn minute! I said, 'Leave 'im 'lone!'* " insisted the man in the T-shirt, his big hands now on his hips, his head thrown back. "I could dig it if he wuz a honkey, but he a brotha, nigguh! He one o' us! Jes keep duh cam'ra an' let 'im go, y'heah?" the man in the T-shirt continued to insist. He duh baddes' o' all dem nigguhs, Fathead thought quickly. Ain' no question 'bout dat!

"Okay, Big Black, okay," said the short, stocky safecracker who was still choking the young man at the collar with a fist full of shirt and tie. Real slowly, he loosened his hands and stepped back, the bitter anger in his glazed eyes fixed permanently, it seemed, on the young man in the blue suit.

"Now you git duh hell on 'way from 'round heah!" Big Black ordered the young man, white spittle spurting from his thick lips. "Dey gon keep yo' cam'ra, but dat's betta'n gittin' fucked up, ain't it? If you'da been a honkey, I wouldn'ta been able t' stop dees nigguhs from stompin' yo' ass—an' prob'ly wouldn'ta wanted to. You lucky you a brotha, nigguh!" Big Black scolded the young man while shaking a firm finger before his face.

The young man said nothing. Slowly, in the noon sun richly ablaze far off in the clear blue distance, he turned and stalked away from expressionless black faces of steel eyes fixed on him. Then, without camera, he hurried off on tired feet to the white Volkswagen parked at the end of the block, around the corner from Doc's. Nervously, he fumbled at the door lock with his key. Once inside the bug of a car, its seats baked by scorching heat from the yellow sun, he was off and quickly out of sight.

"Man, dat wuz somp'n! Whew! Yeah, he lucky he a brotha, ain't he, man?" Boobie said as though he couldn't really believe what he had just witnessed, his big eyes still glued to the corner. "Ahma have me a taste behind dat! You?"

"Really!" was all Fathead could find to say.

THE ROCK OF AGES

Dexter Avenue and Chicago Boulevard. The Corner. Been a long time since I been around here with *these* bloods. Well, see the bar is still there . . . and the muthafucka look the same as it always did: Stonestreet still ain't fixed that rip in the awning and the window Gerald threw that sissy through is still boarded up. Wonder if the same dudes still hang in there. Let me see, . . . there was Fuzz and Okey-Doke . . . and Fast Freddie, wit' his jive self, . . . and who else? Oh, yeah, Peelo, Big Sam, Johnny Mac, Short Dog, Moon Man, Cracker Jack . . . and Red. My man Black Red! Oh, almost forgot about Shaw and Slappy and Snake . . . Shit, there come Red out the bar, now! Still look the same. Wonder if he still got that problem with his stomach. Had to stop drinking. Said he was gon stick to that dynamite "jungle" smoke from now on. That's right, he said that three years ago, before I left here to go to L.A. He look all right to me and he still out here on this corner, so he must be doin' okay.

The car horn from behind jarred my recollections of The Corner and reminded me that the traffic light was now green. I pressed down on the accelerator and charged off, my eyes instinctively glued to the rear-view mirror, a frown on my face. Jes a impatient broad. Where she hurryin' to? Think Ahma shoot on back around there and holler at Red for a minute. I pulled over to the curb and stopped and waited for the slowmoving traffic to clear on both sides of the wide street. Then I swung around quickly, the car's tires squealing in the soft asphalt, and headed to The Corner. Damn, it's been three years since I been gone. Three years! Sho don't seem that long. Course, I s'pose it has been, though, 'cause Blackwell died in seventy-two and ... let me see ... that was the last time I saw Red ... was at the funeral down the street there at McFalls. He was one of the pallbearers. Yeah, Blackwell ... Nevah did stop groggin'. Was deep into it. Shit killed 'im.

"The Corner!" I said aloud to myself as I eased to a stop next to a parking space that really seemed too small for my ride. *Damn!* Well, let me try it, anyway. Seem like it took me five minutes to wiggle and force my way into the tight spot halfway down the block from where Red was now standing in front of the bar at The Corner. He was leaning on a parking meter with his arms folded. The blistering morning sun was now hidden discreetly by a sky of smut gray clouds. Heavy aromas of sweet juicy bar-b-que and deep fried shrimp in the humid mid-afternoon air lured my nostrils as I took in the block.

Soul Wash Laundromat, I noticed as I started walking slowly toward The Corner, was still operating strong. Always did have a pretty good business. Course, I guess it was gon do that, anyway, 'cause it was the only one nearby. And Sister Reed's Missionary Diner look the same, too. Crowded as ever. That's where nigguhs from all over town came to get them hot catfish sandwiches and pig feet dinners . . . and, yeah, them sweet fried pies Sister Reed made at her pad. Sho was good! Damn, what happened to the used car place that was over there next to Meatland? What was the name of it? . . . Yeah, Chappy's Playersville for Wheels. That's it. Nigguh didn't sell nothin' but used Marks and them Hog broughams. Always be talkin' 'bout which pimp or player used to own "dis one" or "dat one" of the rides he had lined up in neat rows on the big lot. Ain't nothin' now but a vacant lot with waist-high weeds and trash and shit everywhere. Sho do look a mess. That's strange . . . Thought Chappy was really makin' it. Maybe he got big time and copped a dealership or something. Nigguh always did brag about how he was "gittin' plenty money" and how he was gon sho 'nough git over one day . . . I stopped and lit a cigarette, my eyes focused on The Corner, where Red was still standing, his chunky body in plain view. Suddenly I dug the Hot Record Man, a stack of lp's tucked under his arm. Tailing him was that little broad that used to whoe real good. They had just come out the bar and were hurrying across Dexter to the gray brick four-family flat on Chicago. Lola? Is that it? Damn, I nevah could remember that broad's name. That's right, she was stretched out on that jones. Always talkin' 'bout what a mellow blow she "jes had." Wudn't but about eighteen or nineteen. Had a heart-shaped gold tooth in the front of her mouth and always smiled so you'd be sure to see it. Said she was from Atlanta. What's her name? Lulu! That's what they called her, with her big wide ass. Didn't look bad in the jib, either. Snake always did say she had some mellow works. Said him and Short Dog freaked-out with her one day around there at his crib on Rochester. Ran a choo-choo on her ass.

    As I got closer to Red, his back to me, I

quickly thought about the time when he and I and the rest of the cats were in the alley behind Stonestreet's Bar there on that hot summer day, drinking the case of Piper-Heidsieck that Gerald stole off the delivery truck in front of the drugstore them Jews owned down the street. Oh, yeah, we was gittin' down! Joe Hughes got drunk as a skunk and put a match to the paper stuffed in the garbage can that that fat rat they called "Tojo" darted into but got his ass out of somehow when them flames started leapin' out. Nevah will forget that! Tojo . . . a baaad muthafucka!

"Red! What it is, my man?" I said as I stepped up to him in the sultry heat of the day.

"Hey, now, whut's hap'nin'?" he returned in a common day-to-day tone, the kind with no real feeling. It was because he didn't recognize me right away. Then, with sudden awareness scrawled on his hard, round face, he questioned me: "School Boy?"

"Yeah, man."

"My man!" He threw out the palm of his hand for me to give him a mop. "I didn't recognize who you wuz wit' dat beard all ov'r yo' face. You ain't done got t' be one o' dem revolution nigguhs, is yuh?" he went on, laughing in his gravelly voice of Black southern flavor and style, his eyes studying my 'fro.

Me, a revolution nigguh? Well, in a sense I guess I am, but not the way Red talkin' 'bout. Hell, throughout history nigguhs ain't nevah really won against whitey in blow-to-blow battle. The riot here in the summer of sixty-seven, and everywhere else in the country, proved that, again. Them police and national guard put the nigguhs in they place in no time. After four or five days of lootin' an' burnin' an' shootin' an' shit, the only thing left as a reminder of "progress" was a bunch of dead bloods and the remains of what looked like a battleground to live in.

"Yeah, I guess I have changed a little, Red," I said, still thinking a bit about what had just crossed my mine. "Been a long time since I been around here."

"Yeah, School Boy, I ain't seen you fo' two o' three years now, since you split an' went to ... er, uh, ... Califo'nia to teach, right?"

"Yeah, that's right. I been teachin' Black lit. courses at Compton Junior College ever since I went out there. Teachin' nigguhs how to try to git theyself together an' *suhvive!*"

"I know you dig it. Plen'y fine broads an' shit..." He smiled.

"Yeah, it's mellow. Here, man," I began, reaching to my hip pocket for my wallet, "let me show you a flick o' the chick I'm stayin' wit' now." I opened to the section with the pictures and, with a fixed smile smeared on my face, said, "Here," handing Red the wallet at the same time. "That's her! Her name is Shana. That's the kinda broads out there." I knew what his reaction was going to be.

"God-t-mighty-knows!" His eyes widened somewhat as he continued to study the photograph exposing clearly Shana's firm breasts and shapely thighs. She was wearing the skimpy bikini she had brought back a year ago from Italy, where she had been studying in an African literature fellowship program at the University of Catania on the island of Sicily. "*Damn!* She sho is stacked! She Black? Look like she mixed wit' a little somp'n ... somp'n foreign ... like a ..."

"Yeah, her mama was Korean an' her daddy was a Black cat overseas in the Army during the fifties."

"Oh, dat's why she look Chinese, hunh?"

"A-ha-ha-ha-ha-ha ... Yeeeeah." Red always did make me laugh. "Course, she act like a nigguh broad, though, Red."

"Thank Ahma go back out dere wit'chu fo' awhile," he kidded with a high-pitched giggle as he handed my wallet back to me. "So you doin' all right, hunh, School Boy?"

"Pretty fair, Red, pretty fair."

"Dat's good, man. Ain't nothin' wrong

wit' dat." He reached into his shirt pocket and pulled out a crooked cigarette which he quickly stuck in the corner of his mouth. "Well, thangs 'bout duh same 'round heah," he continued, the hard nail of his thumb striking fire to the head of a kitchen match.

I took a last deep draw from the cigarette I had lit a few minutes before. Then I dropped the butt on the littered sidewalk and mashed it with the heel of my foot, noticing at the same time the broken bottle of ketchup on the curb to the right of me. The splattered sauce was rolling over the curb, running slowly through the metal grate covering the smelly sewer directly below. It quickly reminded me of the time that dude got shot in the face in the bar there several years ago. Scared the shit outta me. Blood was all over 'im!

"Thangs still the same around here, hunh, Red?" I wondered if anything had really changed at all. "See they done tore down the car lot over there." I imagined the used-to-be glossy Hogs and Marks customized with silver fronts, running boards and soft-padded print tops. "What's Chappy into now? He still sellin' them bad rides?"

"Naw, he in duh graveyard. Dey found 'im dead 'n a *muthafucka* ov'r dere on duh high school playground, quiet as it's kept."

"Really?"

"Yeah, man. Had twelve slugs in 'im. Shot 'im fo' times in duh head! Dat wuz only 'bout a mont' ago."

"What happened?"

"Uh, dey say he wuz dealin' real heavy in dat dope thang an' didn't pay off when he wuz 'pose to."

"Oh, yeah? Who did it?"

"Dey ain't nevah found out. You know how it be when dem kind o' nigguhs git duh rip put to 'em. Duh police don't pay much attention t' dat."

Just at that moment the wailing sound of a police siren erupted on us from two blocks away and began approaching with crisp intensity.

"See dere, dey prob'ly on dey way to a shootin' now, quiet as it's kept," said Red, his outstretched arm pointing to the blue and white car *zoooommin* by us at raceway speed, the brilliant blue light whirling and screaming and whirling and screaming and whirling and screaming in the dullness of the gray day.

Quickly a crackling growl roared out from the sky and pierced my insides like a million dark voices in unison.

"Thank it gon po' down d'rec'ly," Red imagined, the cupped palm of his big hand wiping away the many beads of sweat on his aging forehead. He reared back his head a bit, eyebrows raised, and peered at the thick and sooty clouds hanging almost motionless in the dim distance.

"Yeah, you ain't jeffin' about that," I said, my eyes now off into the same direction Red was still examining. Suddenly the thought of what he had said a few minutes before quickly flashed through my mind again: "So thangs still about the same around here, hunh?"

"Well, thangs done got betta fo' some o' duh nigguhs 'round heah, but, you know, some peoples don't wanna do nothin' no way. See, you got dem kind. Some peoples ain't nevah had a Social Security card in dey life . . . an' don't want one! Dey like what dey doin'."

"I s'pose you right about that. It's the same way out there in L.A."

"Yeah, man, two o' three bottles o' wine a day—dey thank dat's enough. Dey thank dat's livin'!" With the big fingers of his left hand clinging to the top of the parking meter, he parted his legs and bent over. Then, with the thumb of his free hand, he pressed tight against the right side of his nose and snorted out through his left nostril a lumpy stream of greenish snot. I continued to watch him as he reached to his hip pocket for the wrinkled hankie he used to wipe away the bit of stringy mucous still hanging from his wiry mustache.

"Well, dig, Red, you think there's any way to change um . . . you know, make um try to do somethin' for theyself?"

"Might be a way t' change some o' duh young, but you catch duh ol' ones . . . like Rock dere . . . been doin' dat all his life. . . ." He pointed across the street to the run-down red brick apartment house where two Black men, old fellows, were sitting on the first step of the concrete stoop, their crossed legs stretched out on the narrow walkway leading from the entrance to the wide sidewalk cluttered with trash. "He got a pay stub in his pocket from Ford, where duh las' pay he had wuz in nineteen thirty-eight."

"Nineteen thirty-eight?!" I said, turning to Red quickly with a twisted face of total disbelief.

"Yeah, nineteen thirty-eight! He don't wanna do no mo' 'n whut he doin' now, sittin' in dat do' drankin' wine. See 'im sittin' ov'r dere?"

I stared across the street, again. One of the men, I could see clearly, was now guzzling from the mouth of an upturned wine bottle, his Adam's apple sliding up-and-down, up-and-down, up-and-down. His face was hidden somewhat by the turn-down brim of the big black "gangster" hat swallowing his head. That must be Rock, I thought. Darting in and out of the entrance were two little wooly-head boys about seven or eight. They were playing a serious game of "Cops and Robbers" with shiny toy pistols that looked like the real thing. "Bang! Bang! I gotchu! You *dead!*" I heard one boy shout at the other as he ran across the street to hide behind a parked car in front of a small storefront church halfway down the block from where Red and I were standing. Through the screen door of the church, Black gospel voices quickly blared out, slow and steady:

I have a haven when I'm distressed,
I have a refuge when I'm oppressed,
I have a shelter in the time of storm,
I know I'll be safe if I bury myself in Jesus' arms...

They sho gittin' down! I thought. Git to the inside o' yo' *soul!*

"Rock doin' exactly what he wanna do, hunh, Red?"

"Right. Dat's his livin', dat's his life. He jes as happy doin' dat as me an' you would be doin' anythang else."

"That's the same as a job to 'im, hunh?"

"Yeah, he happy like dat. See, fo' dem dat's got ol' an' done did dat all dey life, it ain't no turnin' 'round. But it might be a little help fo' duh young ones," Red determined, a frayed toothpick twirling between his decaying front teeth.

"Yeah, you right, Red, 'cause ... "

Quickly he jumped in without letting me finish what I was about to say:

"Dat's duh troof, School Boy! Some peoples don't wanna do no mo' 'n dey doin' now. You rememba three o' fo' years ago when dey wuz hirin' anybody walked in dem employment offices at dees fact'ries . . . dat *wanted* to work?"

"Yeah, I do."

"Dat wuz jes three o' fo' years ago! If you could lif' anythang, dey'd hire yuh. All dem guys—dey didn't have no job. Dey wuz doin' *exac'ly* what dey doin' now."

"Then, hunh?"

"Yeah, an' ain't went dat way," Red said with a swallow in his voice.

"Ain't went that way, hunh?" I laughed a bit. "You couldn't even come over here an' pick um up everyday an' carry um out there to the job, hunh, Red?"

"Naw. Dey'd find some kind o' excuse fo' not goin'. What dey doin' now is *exac'ly* what they wanna do. Dat's dey life. No turnin' dem ol' ones around. Maybe dem young ones can be turn around. But dem ol' ones—dey *gone!*"

"Ain't no help in sight, hunh?" I said wondering seriously now about what Red was saying.

"Naw. See, Ahm jes tellin' you *exac'ly* what's still hap'nin' 'round heah on dis co'nuh."

Again, a rumbling roar from the dark sky cried out and seemingly shook the concrete sidewalk beneath my feet. Red ignored the jolting sound as he fumbled in his shirt pocket for another cigarette.

"You see," he started, pausing to put the cigarette in his mouth, "it nevah have hurt me, 'cause I awways had a job. I awways wanted t' work. I had t' work 'cause I don't know nothin' else. I ain't got nerve enough t' steal . . . an' peddle dope an' shit like dat. I ain't got dat kinda nerve." He took his hand and wiped away the sweat that had formed again on his forehead. "So, you see, some peoples is made t' hustle . . . an' some peoples is made t' work—an' ev'rybody cain't hustle. Ev'rybody cain't be no hustler. So I wuz jes made t' be a worker. Dat's all. Dat's all I wuz made t' be—a worker. 'Cause if I wuz out heah hustlin' now, I'd stahve t' death!"

"Say you would, Red?" I said with a laugh again.

"Yeah, man, dat's right. Shit, if I go t' steal somp'n, I pick it up an' put it right back down. Look like somebody lookin' at you ev'ry time. So I ain't no thief. I wouldn't make it bein' no hustler, man. All I know is dat I got t' keep on doin' whut Ahm doin' 'til dat man say, 'You done had enough, you sixty-five years ol', an' you go on home an' gitchu some res' an' wait on duh mailman.' An' you only have t' wait five years an' you a dead duck!"

"Ha-ha-ha-ha-ha..." Damn, I thought, Red got about fifteen more years to go! I remembered he was about forty-eight or fifty.

"You ain't gon git a chance t' draw much o' dat money, man! Dey need t' cut dat age down t' 'round fi'ty-five, *anyway*, ... an' twen'y an' out!" He peered at the sky again.

He right about that, I imagined, 'cause Uncle Will died in seventy or seventy-one. That's right, it was in seventy-one—the year after he had retired from working in the foundry at Chrysler's for forty-five years. Musta started there in the mid-twenties 'cause he was sixty-six when he died. Died in his sleep. Didn't git a chance t' draw much o' that money Red was talkin' about. The crowded funeral sho was sad. I can still remember some of the eulogy Reverend Sampson gave on that cool, dreary day at Golgotha Baptist Church:

God said you were getting weary
So He did what He thought best,
He came and stood beside you
And whispered, 'Come and rest.'
You bade no one a last farewell
Not even a goodbye.
You were gone before we knew it
And only God knows why...

And Red went on: "Yeah, twen'y years is enough t' do physical labor like dat, man, lif'in' dat red hot iron. I lif' *hot iron!* Dat iron be duh coluh o' dat car dere when I drag it out dat furnace," Red said, nodding at a bright red Cadillac cruising by, the driver's slanted body supported by the arm rest, his white "godfather" hat cocked on the right side of his fluffy Afro. "See, twen'y years o' dat shit is a *whōle* lot, man!"

"Yeah, I can dig where you comin' from."

"Goddamn right, ... an' dey want thirty an' sixty-five."

"Jones retire yet?"

"Yeah, he retired las' Octoba."

"He sixty-five?" He sho don't look it, I thought.

"Naw. He come out on ... er, uh, ... thirty years."

"Oh, thirty an' out ... Now that's a crazy nigguh there, boy," I said, thinking about the time Jones, drunk as he could be, fell off the bar stool and hopped up and slurred: "Ev'rythang all right! Ah-Ah-Ah-Ahm duh ... duh same one!" Everybody cracked up! Talked about his ass for *days!* Course, it didn't bother him none.

"Who?" said Red, the puzzled look on his round face indicating he was trying to figure out what "crazy nigguh" I was talkin about.

"Jones."

"Yessuh! Well, see, lif'in' iron dat long'll run you crazy. You try lif'in' iron fo' thirty years. Shit, dat's damn near ol' as you is, School Boy."

"I know it. I ain't but thirty-five."

"Dat's jes five years' dif'ence."

"That's right."

"You jes try lif'in' some iron fo' thirty years. See, a nigguh like Jones ain't got no education. He done had duh hardes' jobs out dere an' *suhvived*. He be walkin' 'round actin' a damn fool. I lef' 'im in duh bar las' night cuttin' a fool. He cain't help but act a fool."

"All that iron an' shit done ran 'im crazy, hunh?"

"Yeah, any time you lif' iron thirty years . . . Man, I go home sometime now an' *dreeeam* 'bout dat iron! Dream Ahm out dere lif'in' hot iron . . . wake up . . . be sayin', 'Whew!' " He twisted and turned his burly body to show how he dodged the hot steel in the dreams he had had. "See all dem burns dere?" He stuck out his bare arms in front of him, turning them inside, then outside. "Looka dere. Looka dere. Dat's hot iron. All dat. All dem. Hot iron. All o' dem," he convinced me, pointing from one black scar to another black scar.

"Damn, Red!" I said, surprised to see the many burnt spots on his arms.

"Man, dat iron be duh coluh o' dat shirt dat fat-belly girl dere got on," he stressed again as he brought my attention to the loud red blouse draping the plump pregnancy of a passing teenager. The yellow glitter in her leaf-shaped earrings was accenting the reddish brown dye in her long, pressed hair. "Dat's duh troof, dough, School Boy. Quiet as it's kept, any sonabitch lif' iron thirty years, when he come outta dere he *got* to be crazy! Ain't no question 'bout dat!"

I thought about what Red had been saying as I looked across the street again and saw the old man in the big black hat. Lif'in' that hot iron ain't nothin' but another form of slavery. Modern slavery. Legitimate slavery. Only difference is that now they *do* pay the nigguhs a little bit to do that hard-ass work before they die, or go crazy. We got into a deep rap about this point in the Richard Wright course I taught last semester. It was right at the end of the course, just before I split from L.A. to come back home here for the summer.

"Rock still out there, I see," I said to Red who was now cleaning his grimy nails with the long push-button knife he always carried in his back pocket, where it was "ready fo' me t' trim a nigguh down, if need be."

He looked across the street. "Yeah, dere Rock dere. See dat? He doin' *exac'ly* whut he wanna do, right now. Dat's his job, see. He drawed his las' pay from Ford, he say, in nineteen thirty-eight." He stepped into the street, between two parked cars, and yelled: "Hey, Rock! Come heah!"

Half-startled by the gruff sound of Red's voice, the man in the black hat, now nestled sluggishly in the apartment doorway, raised his drooping head slowly and looked squintingly to where we were standing.

"Come heah!" Red yelled again.

The man nodded his head affirmatively and threw up his arm at the same time. Then, with the palms of his hands pressed against the concrete where he sat, he jacked himself up, stumbling two or three times before he landed on his feet. I watched him with straining eyes as he, gingerly, wobbled slowly out into the wide street. His mouth open, he jerked his head frantically from left to right to scan the swiftly moving cars. Then, as soon as a way became clear, he staggered quickly to the fading white lines dividing the four traffic lanes.

"Stonestreet had 'im sweepin' out duh goddamn bar. He said dat wuz too harda work fo' him," Red said as Rock, widelegged, hurried on across the street, his baggy pants flapping in the soft wind.

Just as Rock stepped up onto the sidewalk, his hand palming tightly the big black hat on his head, Red spoke to him. "Hey, Rock, dat pay stub you got in yo' pocket dere from Ford—you still got it, o' is it done wo' out?"

"In forty-one?"

"It wuz thirty-eight, wudn't it?"

"Naw, forty-one!"

"Dat wuz yo' las' pay stub, hunh?"

"Yeah, dat wuz when I went in duh Ahmy." He shoved his hands into his back pockets and rolled his glassy eyes quizzically.

"Forty-one, hunh? Dat's been a little while, ain't it?" Red continued laughingly.

"Yeeeah..." And Rock laughed, too.

"Stonestreet gave you a job, too, sweepin' out dere in front o' duh thang an' you said dat wuz too hard!"

"Sho wuz!" Quickly Rock threw back his head, his hand palming his hat again, and, through reddish, glassy eyes, inspected the dark sky hovering over us. An ugly scar—running down the side of his frail neck, from his ear lobe to his Adam's apple—stuck out like a puffy, slithery welt received from a severe whipping with a hickory switch. *Damn, how'd that happen?* I thought, my eyes revealing the cringing feeling that quickly ran through me. "Ahma git out dis rain," Rock said as a shrieking clatter of thunder boomed out again. The sound this time was more arresting than before.

"Wait a minute, Rock. Looka heah, you ain't had nothin' since forty-one . . . nair one o' dem yokes?" said Red, continuing to quiz him.

"Naw, naw . . . Goddamn, Ahm fucked up! My back hurt, my leg hurt, . . . my head hurt, . . . my feets hurtin' me an' ev'rythang! Ah ain't gon do a muthafuckin' thang, no mo'!" Rock emphasized, sprays of white spittle spurting from his mouth as he spoke in his shrill voice. With his thumbs he pulled on the elastic straps of his tattered suspenders. Gray bristles stood out on his sunken cheeks like porcupine quills.

"No mo', hunh?"

"No mo'!"

Red continued to tease him. "But you ain't had nair one o' dem jobs since . . . er, uh, . . . dat las'un you had at Ford, is yuh?"

"Hell naw! When duh *ol'* man wuz dere, he worked duh hell outta me. Duh *ol'* man."

"Ol' Henry himself, hunh?" said Red, a smile all over his face.

"Ol' Henry hisself. Dat's right." Rock looked at the sky again, then he said, "Ahm gittin' out dis rain." He turned quickly and squeezed his boyish body between two parked cars. Then, like before, he threw his head from left to right to check the flow of the traffic, and as soon as the chance came, he scurried on across the street. Red and I watched him as he hurried along. In no time, it seemed, he was back in the apartment doorway, sitting humpbacked with locked arms around his propped-up knees, his head drooping.

"Shit, Ahm tellin' you—Rock doin' whut he wanna do...," said Red.

"He doin' *exactly* what he wanna do, hunh, Red?" I said. Quickly I thought: Is Rock really doin' *exactly* what he wanna do?

"He don't like no rain, dough," said Red.

"Yeah, that's what he jes said ..."

"He don't like water."

"He don't like water?" What does Red mean by that?

"No mo' 'n t' drank. He might drank a little, but as far as puttin' some on 'im, he don't care nothin' 'bout dat," Red snickered.

"A-ha-ha-ha-ha-ha-ha-ha-ha-ha ... Red, you kid'n. He ain't gon do that, hunh?"

"Didn't you heah 'im say, 'Ahm gittin' out dis water'? It ain't five drops o' rain fallin' out heah. I thought dat thang had thirty-eight on it, but it wuz forty-one, he said. He went in duh Ahmy in forty-one."

"Well, that's jes as bad!" I said.

"Hell, ain't but two o' three years' dif'ence. Dat's a long time fo' t' be done nevah did nothin'," said Red. He coughed once . . . then twice . . . then three times. I could hear the phlegm gurgling in this throat. "He said he wuz out dere when duh ol' man started duh fac'ry. Said he left 'way from out dere, too!" He coughed again, this time clearing his throat. Then he leaned over and spit on the grate cover of the sewer. The ketchup, I noticed, had stopped rolling over the curb and was now beginning to dry.

"He said duh ol' man worked him, didn't he?" I said.

"Yeah, he said he worked up under 'im, . . . so he musta started dere 'round in duh thirties. Ol' Ford died in duh forties, didn't he?"

"Yeah. But Rock mighta put in 'bout ten o' fifteen years out there. Don'chu think so, Red?"

"Man, Rock ain't worked dat long no where. He mighta had fo' o' five years out dere. He ain't gon work dat long. He ain't duh type dat'd do dat. I tol' you Stonestreet give 'im a lil' job dere where he could make 'im some wine money, sweepin' out dere in front o' duh bar. He thoed dat broom down. He swept up 'bout a day. Next day he carried dat broom back an' give it t' Stonestreet an' said, 'Dat work jes too hard fo' me!'"

"That's what he said, Red!?"

"Yeah. Said it's too hard fo' 'im ... git 'im down in his back an' all dat! Man, Ahm tellin' you—Rock nem is a mess." Quickly he changed the subject. "Boy, you could write a book 'bout dis co'nuh. Dey had a shoot-out ov'r dere in front o' dat service station day befo' yestuhday. Let me see, wuz dat day 'fo' yestuhday? Whut today? Sunday? No, dat wuz Thursday. Dem nigguhs wuz out dere shootin' at each othuh, den dey went on 'round in duh alley an' swopped some lead. One nigguh wuz shootin' a machine gun out dere ... See dat gray brick dere?" He pointed to the four-family flat across the street at the corner, where Lulu and the Hot Record Man had hurried into.

"Over there on the corner? Where that dude is standin' by that cart?"

"Yeah, right dere where dat man sellin' dem hot sausage an' tamales out dat white buggy. Right dere in dat flat. Dat's where it all originated from ... from right dere."

"An' the police was here like flies, hunh?"

"Uh, one police sergeant wuz out dere an' he, ... er, uh, ... wuz ridin' in a car by 'isself. He wuz lookin' at um shootin' at each othuh. He drove down on duh co'nuh o' Joy Road an' got on duh radio an' called. He wudn't gon git in duh line o' fire! He got out from 'round heah. Went down dere on duh co'nuh o' Joy . . . an' aftuh 'while twelve o' thirteen car loads come up heah . . . but all dem guys had got away by den."

"I bet that was somethin', man."

"Really! So you see, School Boy, ain't nothin' changed 'round heah. See, dat's duh reason I call Rock—to let you know I wuz tellin' you duh troof. Rock doin' *exac'ly* what he wanna do, right now! *He livin' right'n duh middle o' duh 'merican dream an' don't eb'n know he sleep!* He triflin', but dat's my nigguh. See, so don't make no dif'ence how good somp'n git, you ain't gon help some peoples. Dey happy duh way dey is, . . . dey like whut dey doin'."

"Ain't no help fo' um, hunh, Red?"

"Naw. If a job come in duh house dere, Rock ain't gon take it. He prob'ly done drunk fo' o' five bottles o' wine dis mawnin."

"Sho 'nough, Red? He drink that wine like it's water, hunh?"

"Yeah, he like wine. Sho 'nough, dough, he done drunk 'bout three fifths," Red corrected himself.

"He ain't gon work no where, hunh, Red?"

"No-o-o-o-o-o-o-o-o-o. . . He ain't gon lif' nothin'. . . "

" 'Cept dat jug, hunh?" I laughed.

"He'll lif' up one o' dem wine bottles, but he ain't gon do nothin' physical."

"He hate work, hunh?"

"Ooooooooooooooooooooooo!!! An' he in a position where he *cain't* hustle. He cain't do none o' dat shit... He cain't do nothin' but whu'chu see 'im doin' dere—sittin' right dere in dat do', drinkin' dat wine an' waitin' on death t' come an' visit his ass!"

Just then jagged streaks of silver accompanied by the crackling of more thunder lashed out from the black cloud hanging above and flashed bright light into the dark day for ten or so fleeting seconds. Then the sky, quickly black again, erupted suddenly with hard beads of stinging rain.

"Ahma do like Rock ov'r dere," Red laughed. "Ahm gittin' out dis rain." He hunched his shoulders and pulled his frayed shirt collar up around the nap of his neck. "You gon be 'round awhile, School Boy?"

"Yeah, for the rest of the summer," I said, backing away from where I had been standing.

"Well, be cool. Dig you tomorrow," said Red as he turned quickly and ran to get under the ripped awning at Stonestreet's Bar.

I turned and sprinted to my car with careful strides. The electrifying downpour was slapping me steadily in my face while

I hurried, clumsily, to unlock the door and jump inside. Quickly I started the motor and turned on the defogger to clear the mist that had formed on the windows. Then I turned on the radio, and out came the powerful, reverent voice of what struck me as a Black preacher deep into his sermon:

"... *an' we've gotta stand an' preach the word, Ha! We need t' git together, Ha! an' git that devil out of our society, Ha! because he's ruinin' us, Ha! he's killin' us, Ha! he's takin' us down-n-n-n* ... Hallelujah. Hallelujah."

Suddenly the heavy downpour changed to hard, icy pellets and began to increase its pounding intensity all over the car. And again streaks of lightning, trailed by the crashing sound of clapping thunder, flashed sporadic brightness into the dim day. *Damn, it's gone to hailin'!* As the blaring voice from the radio went on, I noticed that its rhythmic beat was accompanied magically by the hard-hitting hail stones outside. The sounds of the arrangement caused a pins-and-needles feeling to quickly snake its way from my head to my stomach. Yeah, run yo' thang to um, brotha! Show um where it's at! I lit a cigarette and continued to listen, my ears now tuned in to what the preacher was runnin' down:

"You might not enjoy this kind o' preachin', but there comes a time when we gotta tell it like it is. God put us here for a purpose. An' you know, Ahm jes a little old-fashion, possibly, Ha! Amen, but I *lived* in a home ... where my folks never argued, Ha! before us children, Ha! I know they had differences, Ha! but there was no *arguin'* before the children, Ha! Do y'all hear what Ahm sayin'? *No arguin' before the children! I never saw my father ... strike my mother! I never saw my mother ... strike my father! An' most ...*"

I turned and glanced through the clearing window on the opposite side of the car. Beyond the dense shower blurring my vision a bit, I noticed a white cross on the window of the small storefront church, from where, earlier, I had heard the gospel voices singing about being distressed and oppressed. A faint crimson light behind the ragged yellow curtain at the window revealed vaguely what seemed to be a thin crack running diagonally through the right arm and lower neck of the figure of Jesus painted crudely on the white crisscross symbol.

Suddenly the preacher's sermon was interrupted by the voice of the radio announcer.

"You've been listening to religious services broadcast directly from the Holy Cross Temple of Christ Our Blessed

Savior, 3420 Hastings Street at Brewster, Detroit. The Reverend Moses Story, minister. This is the gospel voice of the Motor City, WJOB, Detroit.

"And now a message from Mr. O. D. Swanson, president of the Swanson Funeral Home, one of Detroit's leading colored undertakers . . ."

Quickly I looked at my wristwatch; the dial showed almost 1:30 p.m. *Damn, time sho do fly by!* I thought as I eased out of the parking space and began creeping along in the street now flooded with giant stagnant puddles my straining eyes fixed on the sheet of rain beating ever-profusely against the windshield. The intensity of the pounding downpour on the top of the car was now more resounding than ever. Once again, a sharp cry from the dark sky screamed out, assaulting my insides, and made my heart flutter. Nervously, I lit another cigarette, and thought:

Yeah, 1:30. Wonder what Shana's doin'. Prob'ly at the beach. Sho was too bad about Chappy. Was really a nice cat. So Jones retired, hunh? He prob'ly *really* actin' a fool now. Poor Rock—jes hangin' on. Doin' *exactly* what he wanna do. "Ha!" And Red . . . "Ha!" Yeah, my man Black Red. Say he go home sometime an' *dreeeam* 'bout dat iron! "Ha!" Still funny as ever. Look a little older now, though . . . Yeah, The Corner. Sunday afternoon.

July twenty-seventh. Nineteen seventy-five. Exactly eight years since sixty-seven. That's right, they gon celebrate the Bicentennial next year. Yeah, they doin' *exactly* what they wanna do!